CONTENTS

Fleet in Focus: British and Continental Steam Ship Co. Ltd. Part 2 *Colin Turner and Roy Fenton*	67
Putting the Record straight	82
Record reviews	85
Beacon Hill *Captain A.W. Kinghorn*	86
The rise and fall of Black Star Line *Peter Newall*	93
Vessels broken up by Arnott, Young at Dalmuir Part 1: 1934-1962 *Ian Buxton*	102
The great cement armada *Malcolm Cranfield*	114
Palm Line's tankers	122
Sources and acknowledgements	126
From the bosun's locker *John Clarkson*	127

Ships in Focus Publications

Correspondence and editorial:
Roy Fenton
18 Durrington Avenue
London SW20 8NT
020 8879 3527
rfenton@rfenton.demon.co.uk

Orders and photographic:
John & Marion Clarkson
18 Franklands, Longton
Preston PR4 5PD
01772 612855
shipsinfocus@btinternet.com

© 2007 Individual contributors, John Clarkson and Roy Fenton.

All rights reserved. No part of this publication may be reproduced, stored in a retrieval system or transmitted in any form or by any means, electronic, mechanical, photocopying, recording or otherwise, without the written permission of the publisher.
Printed by Amadeus Press Ltd., Cleckheaton, Yorkshire.
Designed by Hugh Smallwood, John Clarkson and Roy Fenton.

SHIPS IN FOCUS RECORD
ISBN 978-1-901703-84-9

SUBSCRIPTION RATES FOR RECORD

Readers can start their subscription with any issue, and are welcome to backdate it to receive previous issues.

	3 issues	4 issues
UK	£24	£31
Europe (airmail)	£26	£34
Rest of the world (surface mail)	£26	£34
Rest of the world (airmail)	£31	£41

SHIPS IN FOCUS
November

We take this opportunity to clarify the purpose ~~ ~ ~
It was a title we could not resist, but it seems to have given the impression to some that it exists solely to correct errors. This was never the intention, and as we hoped our readers have made it much more than this, with far more amplification of matters raised than factual correction, as is apparent in almost every issue. We are gratified that features in 'Record' can inspire serious outbreaks of nostalgia amongst readers, which we are happy to hear about and will publish them when we think they are of interest to the readership at large. Yes, corrections do appear, reflecting both the fallibility of editors and that our caption writers and contributors do not necessarily have in depth knowledge of every aspect of shipping. Experts can readily trump them, and when they do so in a courteous manner we are pleased to hear from them. A journal such as this has the advantage over a book that it does not have the last word, and that the record can be put straight in subsequent issues.

Fallibility is in fact a theme of several articles in this issue, as we revisit West Africa. There are ultimately sad accounts of how high hopes for the construction and shipping industries in Nigeria and Ghana were dashed by combinations of economic mismanagement, dictatorship, civil war and corruption. We also tie up a loose end concerning Palm Line's tankers. These vessels were specifically excluded from features in 'Record' 35 and 36, but a reader who served on one has lamented this omission, and we are pleased to rectify it.

John Clarkson   Roy Fenton

One of the many former British ships waiting off Lagos to unload cement at Christmas 1975 was *Nausika*, built by Lithgows Ltd. in 1953 as *Glynafon*. Malcolm Cranfield describes the background to the 'cement armada' from page 114. *[Malcolm Cranfield]*

Matadi Palm of 1948 at Apapa with the tug *Atlas* (1949/500). *[Roy Fenton collection]*

Fulmar was built on the Mersey, at the Garston yard of H. and C. Grayson as *War Yare*, one of five ships ordered by the Shipping Controller. *[Top: Colin Turner collection, bottom: M. Cooper/J. and M. Clarkson]*

Fleet in Focus
BRITISH AND CONTINENTAL STEAM SHIP CO. LTD.
Part 2
Colin Turner and Roy Fenton

Kittiwake (1) in the Mersey (upper) and as the *Cardross* (lower) after her sale to James Patrick of Sydney, Australia along with the *Merganser*. As the *Kittiwake* we see her in the Mersey inward bound for Eastham with her masts lowered ready for her passage up the Manchester Ship Canal. She was the first ship built for Cork Steamship after the First World War. [Upper: B. and A. Feilden/Nigel Farrell collection: lower: Ian J. Farquhar collection]

10. FULMAR 1922-1927
O.N. 143179 1,698g 1,006n
265.0 x 41.2 x 18.8 feet
T. 3-cyl. by David Rollo and Sons, Liverpool; 201 NHP, 1,100 IHP, 10.5 knots.
1.2.1919: Launched by H. and C. Grayson Ltd., Garston (Yard No. 106).
1.5.1919: Registered in the ownership of the Shipping Controller (Harry S. Reid, manager), London as WAR YARE.
2.8.1919: Sold to the Cork Steamship Co. Ltd., Cork.
1919: Renamed FULMAR.
20.9.1922: Owners became the British and Continental Steamship Co. Ltd., Liverpool.
28.3.1927: Sunk following a collision in fog with the British steamer RIO CLARO (4,086/1922) about three miles south west of Dungeness whilst on a voyage from Liverpool to Rotterdam with general cargo.
5.4.1927: Register closed.

11. KITTIWAKE (1) 1922-1935
O.N. 135724 1,896g 982n
301.0 x 42.5 x 18.9 feet
T. 3-cyl. by Swan, Hunter and Wigham Richardson and Co. Ltd., Newcastle-upon-Tyne; 318 NHP, 1,350 IHP, 11 knots.
29.7.1919: Launched by Swan, Hunter and Wigham Richardson and Co. Ltd., Neptune Works, Low Walker, Newcastle-upon-Tyne (Yard No. 1080).
23.8.1919: Registered in the ownership of the Cork Steamship Co. Ltd., Cork as KITTIWAKE.
12.9.1922: Owners became the British and Continental Steamship Co. Ltd., Liverpool.
30.7.1935: Sold to James Patrick and Co. (Pty.) Ltd., Sydney, New South Wales.
11.10.1935: Renamed CARDROSS.
14.12.1940: In collision with the Australian steamer FIONA (2,198/1933), taken in tow but sank in position 34.07 south by 151.32 east whilst on a voyage from Sydney to Melbourne with general cargo

67

12. MERGANSER (1) 1922-1935
O.N. 135725 1,876g 946n
290.0 x 42.5 x 18.8 feet
T. 3-cyl. by Swan, Hunter and Wigham Richardson and Co. Ltd., Newcastle-upon-Tyne; 318 NHP.
10.10.1919: Launched by Swan, Hunter and Wigham Richardson and Co. Ltd., Neptune Works, Low Walker, Newcastle-upon-Tyne (Yard No. 1135).
15.11.1919: Registered in the ownership of the Cork Steamship Co. Ltd., Cork as MERGANSER.
9.1922: Owners became the British and Continental Steamship Co. Ltd., Liverpool.
1935: Sold to James Patrick and Co. (Pty) Ltd., Sydney, New South Wales and renamed CARLISLE.
1956: Sold to Cambay Prince Steamship Co. Ltd. (John Manners and Co., managers), Hong Kong and renamed TWEED BREEZE.
1961: Transferred to the San Jeronimo Steamship Co. S.A., Panama (John Manners and Co. Ltd., Hong Kong, managers) and renamed SAN JERONIMO.
1962: Broken up in Hong Kong.

13. BITTERN (1)/IMBER (2) 1922-1954
O.N. 143483 1,899g 939n
290.4 x 42.6 x 19.0 feet
T. 3-cyl. by Swan, Hunter and Wigham Richardson and Co. Ltd., Newcastle-upon-Tyne; 318 NHP, 1,350 IHP, 11 knots.
17.6.1920: Launched by Swan, Hunter and Wigham Richardson and Co. Ltd., Neptune Works, Low Walker, Newcastle-upon-Tyne (Yard No. 1116).
20.9.1920: Registered in the ownership of the Cork Steamship Co. Ltd., Cork as BITTERN.

Top: *Merganser* (1). *[Colin Turner collection]*
Above: *Merganser* as *Carlisle,* after sale to Australia and some modifications. *[Ian J. Farquhar]*
Below: The first *Bittern* in the Mersey. Note the deck cranes. A post-war view as *Imber* (2) shows that her bridge structure has been modified (opposite top). She was renamed at the request of the Admiralty, to avoid confusion with HMS *Bittern*. *[Below: B. and A. Feilden/J. and M. Clarkson; opposite top: Roy Fenton collection]*

Photographed at sea, *Vanellus* was a sister of *Bittern* (1). The aerial view above shows her deck cranes and that her accommodation was modified post-war with the forward alleyway enclosed. *[Colin Turner collection]*

14. VANELLUS 1922-1954
O.N. 145128 1,896g 1,631n
290.0 x 42.5 x 18.8 feet
T. 3-cyl. by Swan, Hunter and Wigham Richardson and Co. Ltd., Newcastle-upon-Tyne; 318 NHP, 1,350 IHP, 11 knots.
1.9.1920: Launched by Swan, Hunter and Wigham Richardson Ltd., Southwick, Sunderland (Yard No. 1155).
6.1.1921: Registered in the ownership of the Cork Steamship Co. Ltd., Cork as VANELLUS.
12.9.1922: Owners became the British and Continental Steamship Co. Ltd., Liverpool.
27.5.1954: Arrived at Port Glasgow to be broken up by Smith and Houston Ltd.
3.2.1955: Register closed.

20.9.1922: Owners became the British and Continental Steamship Co. Ltd., Liverpool.
29.3.1940: Renamed IMBER.
14.9.1954: Arrived at Antwerp to broken up by Cia. Cinda S.A.
17.9.1954: Register closed.

15. LESTRIS (1) 1922-1936
O.N. 146088 1,881g 937n
290.0 x 42.6 x 18.1 feet
T. 3-cyl. by Swan, Hunter and Wigham Richardson Ltd., Newcastle-upon-Tyne; 318 NHP, 11½ knots.
7.2.1921: Launched by Swan, Hunter and Wigham Richardson Ltd., Neptune Yard, Low Walker, Newcastle-upon-Tyne (Yard No. 1118).
1.9.1921: Registered in the ownership of the Cork Steamship Co. Ltd., Cork as LESTRIS.
9.1922: Owners became the British and Continental Steamship Co. Ltd., Liverpool.
1936: Sold to James Patrick and Co. (Pty.) Ltd., Sydney, New South Wales and renamed CARADALE.
1959: Sold to Far East Metal Industry and Shipping Co. Ltd., Hong Kong.
1.1959: Breaking up began by owners.

Lestris (1) has just entered the Manchester Ship Canal (top), and it appears that she has telescopic topmasts which have been lowered. She reverted to the split-superstructure design of *Kittiwake*. Sold to Australia as *Caradale* (lower), she was substantially modified. *[Upper: J. and M. Clarkson, lower: Ian J. Farquhar collection]*

16. OUSEL 1922-1957
O.N. 1462271 539g 647n
271.3 x 39.1 x 16.6 feet
T. 3-cyl. by Ferguson Brothers (Port Glasgow) Ltd., Port Glasgow; 11 knots, 273 NHP.
1.11.1921: Launched by Ferguson Brothers (Port Glasgow) Ltd., Port Glasgow (Yard No. 262).
10.1.1922: Completed for the Cork Steamship Co. Ltd., Cork as OUSEL.
9.1922: Owners became the British and Continental Steamship Co. Ltd., Liverpool.
8.1.1957: Sank following a collision with the Panama-registered tanker LIVERPOOL (14,539/1922) whilst anchored between Tranmere and New Ferry in the River Mersey during a voyage from Antwerp to Manchester with steel and general cargo.

17. RALLUS 1922-1954
O.N. 147180 1,871g 920n
290.0 x 42.5 x 17.9 feet
T. 3-cyl. by Swan, Hunter and Wigham Richardson Ltd., Newcastle-upon-Tyne; 318 NHP, 1,350 IHP, 11 knots.
1.3.1922: Launched by Swan, Hunter and Wigham Richardson Ltd., Southwick, Sunderland (Yard No. 1167).
28.12.1922: Registered in the ownership of the British and Continental Steamship Co. Ltd., Liverpool as RALLUS.
24.5.1954: Register closed on sale to Compania de Navigation Arcoul S.A., Panama (Emmanuel N. Vintiadis, Genoa, Italy) (Marcou and Sons, London, agents) and renamed GEORGIOS S. under the Costa Rican flag.
1959: Transferred to Compania de Navigation Corthion S.A., Panama (Emmanuel N. Vintiadis, Genoa) (Marcou and Sons, London, agents).
1961: Sold to Lanena Shipping Co. Ltd., Hong Kong (T. Engan, Manila, Philippines) and renamed MIKE under the Panama flag.
1962: Sold to Keanyew Shipping Co. S.A., Hong Kong (Barreto Shipping and Trading Co. Ltd., Singapore) and renamed GITANA under the Panama flag.
1964: Sold to Gilbert Yim Fai Hung (Chan Wing Fai), Hong Kong and renamed FOLK ON under the Panama flag.
12.6.1966: Left Hong Kong for Whampoa to be broken up.

Cork Steamship deserted Swan, Hunter for Ferguson when ordering *Ousel* (above). She has a combination of derricks and deck cranes, and in this aerial view carries a large case on deck. She was the company's last loss (right), sinking after a collision on the Mersey in 1957.

Photographed on the Mersey, *Rallus* (below) was a sister of *Kittiwake* (1) and *Lestris* (1). She was the first vessel delivered to British and Continental.
[Above and right: Colin Turner collection, below: B. and A. Feilden/J. and M. Clarkson]

71

Tringa was the first ship ordered by the new company, and represented a brief flirtation with Dutch shipbuilders. *[B. and A. Feilden/J. and M. Clarkson]*

18. TRINGA 1925-1940
O.N. 147303 1,930g 972n
290.5 x 43.1 x 19.1 feet
T. 3-cyl. by Burgerhout Engineering Works and Shipbuilding Co. Ltd., Rotterdam, Netherlands; 335 NHP, 1,600 IHP, 11 knots
4.1925: Completed by C. van der Giessen en Zonen's Scheepswerft N.V., Krimpen-aan-der-Ijssel, Netherlands (Yard No. 519).
24.3.1925: Registered in the ownership of the British and Continental Steamship Co. Ltd., Liverpool.
11.5.1940: Torpedoed and sunk by the German submarine U 9 about 1.5 miles from the West Hinder light in position 51.21 north by 02.25 east whilst on a voyage from Antwerp to Glasgow with a cargo of potash and iron ore. Sixteen of the crew and the Belgian pilot were lost, the survivors being rescued by HMS MALCOLM and taken to Ramsgate.
16.5.1940: Register closed.

19. PANDION 1926-1941
O.N. 149610 1,944g 999n
291.2 x 43.2 x 19.1 feet
T. 3-cyl. by D. and W. Henderson Co. Ltd., Meadowbank, Glasgow; 334 NHP, 2,000 IHP, 12.75 knots.
21.10.1926: Launched by the Burntisland Shipbuilding Co. Ltd., Burntisland (Yard No. 139).
29.11.1926: Registered in the ownership of the British and Continental Steamship Co. Ltd., Liverpool as PANDION.
28.1.1941: Damaged by German aircraft off the coast of Donegal in position 55.34 north by 10.22 west whilst on a voyage from the Tyne to Leixoes.
30.1.1941: Beached, broke in two and sank in Lough Swilly.
20.2.1941: Register closed

Pandion was British and Continental's first ship from Burntisland and repeated the combination of derricks and deck cranes seen on *Ousel*. *[B. and A. Feilden/J. and M. Clarkson]*

Built and originally owned in Sweden, Serula had a particularly tall funnel. *[Colin Turner collection]*

20. SERULA 1926-1954
O.N. 149591 1,630g 785n
276.0 x 41.2 x 16.0 feet
T. 3-cyl. by Aktiebolaget Finnboda Varv, Stockholm, Sweden; 270 NHP, 1,400 IHP, 10½ knots.
6.1918: Completed by Aktiebolaget Finnboda Varv, Stockholm (Yard No. 302) for Rederi A/B Svenska Lloyd (H. Metcalfe), Göteborg, Sweden as HOLMIA.
7.6.1926: Registered in the ownership of the British and Continental Steamship Co. Ltd., Liverpool as SERULA.
30.9.1954: Register closed on sale to Hellenic Mediterranean Lines Co. Ltd., Piraeus, Greece and renamed ROMELIA.

1956: Sold to Umberto d'Amato (Palomba e d'Amato), Torre del Greco, Italy and renamed CUPIDO.
1961: Renamed AIACE PRIMO.
30.1.1963: Wrecked on Cape Shabla, near Varna whilst on a voyage from Monopoli to Constanza in ballast.

21. DAFILA 1927-1943
O.N. 149657 1,940g 969n
291.5 x 43.2 x 19.1 feet
T. 3-cyl. by D. and W. Henderson and Co. Ltd., Meadowbank, Glasgow; 305 NHP, 1,900 IHP, 11 knots.

8.12.1927: Launched by D. and W. Henderson and Co. Ltd., Meadowbank, Glasgow (Yard No. 816).
2.1.1928: Registered in the ownership of the British and Continental Steamship Co. Ltd., Liverpool as DAFILA.
18.3.1943: Torpedoed and sunk by the German submarine U 593 off Derna, Libya in position 32.59 north by 22.21 east whilst on a voyage from Tripoli to Alexandria with a cargo of empty drums and engines for repair. Nineteen of the crew and three gunners were lost, the survivors being rescued by the armed whaler HMSAS SOUTHERN MAID.
6.4.1943: Register closed.

As well as deck cranes and conventional derricks, Dafila had a heavy-lift derrick at number 2 hold. *[Colin Turner collection]*

22. TADORNA 1928-1942
O.N. 149677 1,947g 984n
291.7 x 43.2 x 19.1 feet
T. 3-cyl. by the Burntisland Shipbuilding Co. Ltd., Burntisland; 305 NHP, 1,900 IHP, 12.75 knots.
21.4.1928: Launched by the Burntisland Shipbuilding Co. Ltd., Burntisland (Yard No. 147).
30.5.1928: Registered in the ownership of the British and Continental Steamship Co. Ltd., Liverpool as TADORNA.
9.11.1942: Captured by Vichy French warships 1½ miles north of Bizerta whilst on a voyage from Glasgow to Malta with food and government stores.
11.1942: Seized by German forces, transferred to Mittelmeer Reederei G.m.b.H. and renamed BALZAC.
7.3.1943: Sunk by United States aircraft 20 miles north north east of Zembra Island, Gulf of Tunis.
10.6.1943: Register closed.

23. NYROCA (2) 1935-1942/1946-1950
O.N. 141873 786g 322n
200.4 x 30.7 x 19.1 feet
T. 3-cyl. by William Beardmore and Co. Ltd., Coatbridge, Glasgow; 115 NHP, 850 IHP, 10 knots
1956: Oil engine 6-cyl. 4SCDA built 1943 by Maschinenbau Augsburg-Nürnberg, Augsburg, Germany.
5.10.1917: Launched by the Ardrossan Dry Dock and Shipbuilding Co. Ltd., Ardrossan (Yard No. 269).
3.1.1918: Registered in the ownership of J. and P. Hutchison Ltd., Glasgow as PHILOTIS.

Above: Tadorna was a sister to Pandion. [B. and A. Feilden/J. and M. Clarkson]
Below: Nyroca, bought from Moss Hutchison in 1935. [Colin Turner collection]

10.3.1934: Owners became the Moss Hutchinson Line Ltd., Liverpool.
7.10.1935: Acquired by the British and Continental Steamship Co. Ltd., Liverpool.
14.10.1935: Renamed NYROCA.
1942: Chartered by the British Government Charter, Salvage and Repair Service.
28.10.1942: Renamed SIR WALTER VENNING.
30.5.1946: Renamed NYROCA following return to owners.
7.11.1950: Register closed on sale to the Somerton Steamship Co. Ltd., San Jose, Costa Rica and renamed ALICE MARIE.
1956: Sold to Michael C. Sorottos, Piraeus, Greece and renamed MAIROULA.
1956: Fitted with an oil engine.
9-10.1974: Broken up at Perama, Greece by Kyriazis Brothers Metalemboriki.

24. DOTTEREL (2) 1936-1941
O.N. 164306 1,385g 580n
262.0 x 40.0 x 15.7 feet
T. 3-cyl. by Rankin and Blackmore Ltd., Greenock; 164 NHP, 1,250 IHP, 11 knots.
17.10.1936: Launched by the Burntisland Shipbuilding Co. Ltd., Burntisland (Yard No. 205).
20.11.1936: Registered in the ownership of the British and Continental Steamship Co. Ltd., Liverpool as DOTTEREL.
7.3.1941: Torpedoed by an E-boat of the German 1st S-Flotille off No. 6 Buoy, Southwold whilst on a voyage from London to Hull and Dublin with general cargo and sank in position 52.41 north by 01.59 east.
21.3.1941: Register closed.

The short-lived *Dotterel* (1). *[Colin Turner collection]*

25. EGRET (2) 1937-1957
O.N. 164316 1,391g 583n
264.0 x 40.0 x 15.7 feet
T. 3-cyl. by Rankin and Blackmore Ltd., Greenock; 144 NHP.
12.3.1937: Launched by the Burntisland Shipbuilding Co. Ltd., Burntisland (Yard No. 206).
8.3.1937: Registered in the ownership of the British and Continental Steamship Co. Ltd., Liverpool as EGRET.
1957: Sold to African Coasters (Pty.) Ltd. (Grindrod, Gersigny and Co. (Pty.), Ltd.), Durban, South Africa and renamed REEF.
1966: Sold to Timor Navigation Corporation S.A., Panama (Lay San Ing, Dili, Timor) and renamed AINARO.
5.1967: Sold and renamed KIEN LOONG.
10.1967: Broken up in Hong Kong by Yuen Hing Hardware Co.

Egret (2) (middle) had a distinctive profile, with one hatch on the forecastle and an extensive outfit of derricks on her two masts, plus deck cranes. *[Roy Fenton collection]*
Reef (bottom) as *Egret* became, at Cape Town in May 1959. *[J. and M. Clarkson collection]*

26. KITTIWAKE (2)   1946-1955
O.N. 181015 2,016g 841n
308.0 x 43.2 x 17.4 feet
T. 3-cyl. by David Rowan and Co. Ltd., Glasgow; 429 NHP, 1,600 IHP, 11.75 knots.
19.12.1945: Launched by the Burntisland Shipbuilding Co. Ltd., Burntisland (Yard No. 299).
7.3.1946: Registered in the ownership of the British and Continental Steamship Co. Ltd., Liverpool as KITTIWAKE.
3.8.1955: Register closed on sale to Hellenic Lines Ltd. (P. G. Callimanopulos), Piraeus, Greece and renamed GERMANIA.
1977: Sold to Wadih Nseir (Sea Transport Agency), Lattakia, Syria and renamed HANAN.
1982: Renamed HANAN STAR.
1988: Reportedly broken up.

First post-war addition to the fleet was *Kittiwake* (2) from Burntisland, a development of that yard's *Egret* (2) with a larger accommodation block (top and middle). She was renamed *Germania* on sale to Greece in 1955 (bottom). *[Top and middle: Colin Turner collection, bottom: J. and M. Clarkson collection]*

27. LESTRIS (2) 1946-1955
O.N. 181027 2,025g 847n
308.0 x 43.2 x 17.4 feet
T. 3-cyl. by Rankin and Blackmore Ltd., Greenock; 226 NHP; 1,500 NHP, 11.75 knots.
5.2.1946: Launched by Hall, Russell and Co. Ltd., Aberdeen (Yard No. 789).
8.7.1946: Registered in the ownership of the British and Continental Steamship Co. Ltd., Liverpool as LESTRIS.
3.8.1955: Register closed on sale to Hellenic Lines Ltd. (P.G. Callimanopulos), Piraeus, Greece and renamed BELGION.
9.4.1968: Stranded off Tripoli, Libya whilst on a voyage from Antwerp to Alexandria and Lattakia with general cargo. Refloated next day and later declared a constructive total loss.
7.9.1968: Arrived at Sveti Kajo, Split to be broken up by Brodospas.

Lestris (2) was a sister to *Kittiwake* (2), although from a different yard. *[Roy Fenton collection]*

28. MERGANSER (2) 1946-1947
O.N. 181034 2,024g 848n
308.0 x 43.2 x 17.4 feet
T. 3-cyl. by David Rowan and Co. Ltd., Glasgow; 429 NHP, 1,600 IHP, 11.75 knots.
14.6.1946: Launched by the Burntisland Shipbuilding Co. Ltd., Burntisland (Yard No. 306).
26.8.1946: Registered in the ownership of the British and Continental Steamship Co. Ltd., Liverpool.
28.4.1947: Sank following a collision with the United States steamer NORWALK VICTORY (1945/7,078) near Doel in the River Scheldt whilst on a voyage from Liverpool to Antwerp with general cargo. There was one casualty.
26.10.1948: Refloated and towed to Antwerp. Later declared a constructive total loss.
4.6.1947: Register closed.
1948: Abandoned to salvors, Enterprises Jos de Smedt, Antwerp, Belgium and repaired for their account by Cockerill, Hoboken.
1950: Returned to service as JEF DE SMEDT.
1951: Sold to Partrederiet Candida (I.A. Hamre and J. Lydersen, managers), Oslo, Norway and renamed CANDIDA.
1960: Sold to A/S Jensen's Rederi I, II, III & IV (Marlow Wangen & Petter Christensen, managers), Arendal, Norway.
1964: Sold to Eurafrican Transport Corporation (Overland Trust Bank), Lugano, Switzerland and renamed ARENDAL under the Liberian flag.
1968: Transferred to Seafoam Shipping Inc. (Overland Trust Bank), Lugano and renamed GEMMA under the Liberian flag.
1974: Sold to Mania Maritime and Commercial Corporation (International Chartering and Shipping Co.) Piraeus, and renamed MANIA under the Liberian flag.
5.8.1971: Abandoned after catching fire 10 miles south west of Bar during a voyage from Piraeus to Venice with a cargo of cotton.
8.8.1971: Ran aground near Split.
11.1974: Broken up at Sveti Kajo, Split by Brodospas.

Merganser, just after her launch at Burntisland. *[Colin Turner collection]*

The *Merganser* (2), on which Colin Turner's father was lost (top). She was another sister of *Kittiwake*. She is also seen in Swiss ownership but under the Liberian flag as *Arendal* (middle).
[Both: Colin Turner collection]

Dundee (below) later became *Dotterel*. *[J. and M. Clarkson collection]*

29. DOTTEREL (3) 1948-1961
O.N. 144713 1,494g 583n
283.8 x 42.3 x 15.8 feet
T. 3-cyl. by Alexander Stephen and Sons Ltd., Linthouse, Glasgow; 361 NHP, 12.5 knots.
28.12.1933: Launched by the Caledon Shipbuilding and Engineering Co. Ltd., Dundee (Yard No. 345).
16.2.1934: Registered in the ownership of the Dundee, Perth and London Steamship Co. Ltd., Dundee as DUNDEE.
5.1948: Acquired by British and Continental Steamship Co. Ltd., Liverpool and renamed DOTTEREL.
28.8.1961: Arrived at Bilbao, Spain to be broken up by A.F. Ondas.

30. ARDETTA 1949-1965
O.N. 182473 1,542g 586n
289.2 x 42.8 x 17.2 feet
T. 3-cyl. by Cammell Laird and Co. Ltd., Birkenhead; 13 knots.
20.12.1948: Launched by Cammell Laird and Co. Ltd., Birkenhead (Yard No. 1193).
19.2.1949: Registered in the ownership of the British and Continental Steamship Co. Ltd., Liverpool as ARDETTA.
1965: Sold to Zade Shipping Co. Ltd., London (Maldivian Nationals Trading Corporation (Ceylon) Ltd., Colombo, Ceylon) and renamed OCEAN PRINCESS.
1970: Transferred to the Far East Shipping and Trading Co. Ltd., Hong Kong (Maldivian Nationals Trading Corporation (Ceylon) Ltd., Colombo, Ceylon) under the Maldives flag.
1975: Managers became Maldives Shipping Ltd., Male, Maldives.
17.4.1976: Arrived at Karachi.
21.4.1976: Sold to Pakistani shipbreakers.
5.1976: Breaking up began at Gadani Beach.

Dotterel (3) was bought from the Dundee, Perth and London Company in 1948. As *Dundee* she spent the years 1943 to 1945 in service with the Admiralty and made 13 Atlantic voyages as a convoy rescue ship. *[Colin Turner collection]*

Ardetta was the first of three near-sisters from Cammell Laird at Birkenhead (middle and bottom). *[Both: Colin Turner collection]*

31. BITTERN (2) 1949-1966
O.N. 183746 1,527g 580g
289.9 x 42.8 x 15.2 feet
T. 3-cyl. by Cammell Laird and Co. Ltd., Birkenhead; 13 knots.
28.6.1949: Launched by Cammell Laird and Co. Ltd., Birkenhead (Yard No. 1194).
1.9.1949: Registered in the ownership of the British and Continental Steamship Co. Ltd., Liverpool as BITTERN.
1966: Sold to Maldives Investments (London) Ltd., London (Maldivian Nationals Trading Corporation (Ceylon) Ltd., Colombo, Ceylon) and renamed MALDIVE EXPRESS under the British flag.
1970: Owners became Maldives Shipping Ltd., Male, Maldive Islands (Maldivian Nationals Trading Corporation (Ceylon) Ltd., Colombo, Ceylon).
21.9.1975: Arrived at Karachi.
Around 29.10.1975: Arrived at Gadani Beach to be broken up.

The Cammell Laird sisters were a development of the Burntisland design without the hatch on the forecastle. This is *Bittern* (2). The company's houseflag appeared as a stem badge. *[Colin Turner collection]*

Completed in 1954, *Clangula* was amongst the last steam-reciprocating engined ships built. *[Colin Turner collection]*

32. CLANGULA 1954-1965
O.N. 185479 1,550g 575n
288.9 x 42.8 x 17.2 feet
T. 3-cyl. by Cammell Laird and Co. (Shipbuilders and Engineers) Ltd., Birkenhead; 1,525 IHP, 13 knots.
23.11.1953: Launched by Cammell Laird and Co. (Shipbuilders and Engineers) Ltd., Birkenhead (Yard No. 1253).
22.2.1954: Registered in the ownership of the British and Continental Steamship Co. Ltd., Liverpool as CLANGULA.
1965: Sold to Ambassadors Steamship Private Ltd. (F. Collis and Co.), Cochin, India and renamed EFFIGYNY.

1969: Owners became Collis Line Private Ltd., Cochin.
5.1979: Reported under arrest at Bombay for non payment of port and other charges.
18.4.1980: Dragged anchor and grounded east of Mazagon in position 18.58 north by 72.52 east. The wreck was reported sold to ship breakers in 1983.

33. EGRET (3)/TARTAR PRINCE 1959-1972
O.N. 301288 1,187g 465g
249.4 x 39.8 x 13.6 feet
8-cyl. 4SCSA oil engine by Klöckner-Humboldt-Deutz AG, Koln, West Germany; 13 knots.
16.10.1958: Launched by Travewerft GmbH, Lübeck, West Germany (Yard No. 226).
1.1959: Completed for the British and Continental Steamship Co. Ltd., Liverpool as EGRET.
1969: Time chartered to Prince Line and renamed TARTAR PRINCE.
1972: Sold to Surveyor Shipping Inc., Panama (Heerema Engineering Service BV, Leiden, Netherlands), converted into a survey ship and renamed SURVEYOR.
4.7.1987: Arrived at Gadani Beach.
9.7.1987: Breaking up began by G.N. Brothers, Gadani Beach.

The German-built motor ship *Egret* (3) was an open shelter decker, with a removable partition in the middle of number 2 hatch which made her effectively a three hatch ship. The accommodation for her crew was described as spacious. It is interesting that no fewer than three of the nineteen crew were catering staff. She is seen as *Egret* (top) and during almost three years on charter to Manchester Prince Line as *Tartar Prince*, during which time she continued to use the Ship Canal whilst running to the Mediterranean (middle), and as the survey ship *Surveyor* (bottom). *[Top: Colin Turner collection, middle and bottom: J. and M. Clarkson]*

Derivation of names

British and Continental continued Cork Steamship's long tradition of giving its ships the names of birds, mainly but not exclusively waterfowl. They were an eclectic mixture, with well-known English names such as *Cormorant* and *Egret* used alongside some scientific names like *Clangula* and *Pandion* which even experienced birders would hardly know. Indeed, a number of these names have been replaced and are absent from present-day bird books.

Ardetta	The scientific name formerly given to species of bitterns (q.v.).
Avocet	An elegant black-and-white wader with a distinctive up-turned bill, notable for having recolonised the United Kingdom since the Second World War.
Bittern	A skulking brown marsh bird related to herons and egrets, more often identified by its booming call than being seen.
Clangula	Scientific name for the long-tailed duck, which breeds on the tundra and winters at sea.
Cormorant	A widespread, fish-eating seabird which characteristically perches with its wings partly open.
Dafila	Former scientific name for the pintail, a duck with a long, pointed tail.
Dotterel	A summer visitor to Europe, an attractive wader which nests high on mountains.
Egret	Predominantly white marsh birds, once shot in huge numbers to provide plumes for ladies' dresses.
Fulmar	A North Atlantic seabird of the petrel family which flies with stiff, straight wings.
Harelda	An American duck known as old squaw, found in some European collections of waterfowl.
Imber	The great northern diver is known as the imber goose.
Jabiru	A name for various species of stork, especially those found in South America.
Kittiwake	An Atlantic gull, much less common inland than other species.
Lestris	Former scientific name for the skua family: fierce, piratical birds which prey on other seabirds and force them to disgorge food.
Merganser	A large duck, equally at home on coastal waters or inland rivers.
Nyroca	The ferruginous duck has the latin name *Aythya nyroca*
Ousel	The ring ousel is a relative of the blackbird living at higher altitudes, distinguished by a white, crescent-shaped mark on its breast,.
Pandion	Latin name for the osprey, a large, fishing-eating bird of prey.
Rallus	This genus includes the water rail, a shy, reed-bed dweller related to the coot and moorhen.
Serula	Also spelt serrula, this is an old name for the red-breasted merganser.
Tadorna	The shelduck, a boldly-marked duck common on coasts, belongs to this genus.
Tringa	The genus which includes a number of species of sandpipers, birds of the shore and inland waters.
Vanellus	Best known member of this genus is the lapwing, also known as the peewit or green plover, a formerly common bird of coastal pastures and farmland, and the source of plovers' eggs.
Whimbrel	A long-billed wader, similar to but smaller than the more familiar curlew.

PUTTING THE RECORD STRAIGHT

Letters, additions, amendments and photographs relating to features in *any* issues of 'Record' are welcomed. Communications by e-mail are acceptable, but senders are asked to include their postal address. Letters may be lightly edited.

Department of correction
Arild ('Record' 36, page 207) does in fact have a raised quarter deck, possibly not as high as some. Note the freeing ports in the bulwarks abreast number 1 hatch and the deck level. Abreast number 2 hatch she is fitted with rails rather than bulwarks which makes the step in the deck less obvious, only being as high as the well deck bulwarks.

Regarding the photograph of the *Seal* on page 46 of 'Record' 37, does anyone know the purpose of the large ring hanging at her stem; was it peculiar to this ship or this company; or a requirement for the trade up the Manchester Ship Canal? It was possibly a towing pennant but the ring seems huge.
CAPTAIN JOHN ANDERSON, 523 Louise Road, Ladysmith, British Columbia, V9G 1W7, Canada

I refer to the caption on page 214, 'Record' 36: '*Loch Etive* in the Avon; note the furled *foresail.*' I would suggest that we should be noting the furled staysail, or maybe the furled topmast staysail, or to be nearer your version a furled forestaysail. A foresail is a term for the main sail set on the foremast - or the fore course - which the *Loch Etive* does not have the main yard to set it on.
FRED KILGOUR, 21 Meiriadog Road, Colwyn Bay LL29 9NR

Congratulations on a fine 'Record' 37 – I loved the Manchester Ship Canal pictures in particular. I was looking at the histories of the various ships of British and Continental and noticed that *Imber* (page 8), which became the Italian *Citta di Bergano*, was down as sunk by HM Submarine *Undaunted* on 14th March 1943. *Undaunted* was herself sunk on or about 13th May 1941. I suggest that the submarine that did the damage was HMS *Unbending*.
BRENT CHAMBERS, Auckland, New Zealand

Comments on coasters
Further to the letters in 'Record' 36 the following comments might be of interest and add to the discussion.
Loch Etive
It is more likely that this vessel was a typical semi-standardised product of Scott and Sons of Bowling as the Caledonian Canal at the time of her build was advertising to take ships of 160 feet overall length and 38 feet overall breadth. Indeed, J. and A. Gardner's *Saint Modan*, built in the same year by Scott and Sons, has almost identical dimensions to *Loch Etive* as well as sharing the same engine builder. In 1905 Scott and Sons built *Clydesdale* for David MacBrayne and she was designed to fit the length of the Caledonian Canal locks as she was intended for the Glasgow to Inverness passenger/cargo trade although it is doubtful if she ever visited Inverness more than two or three times.
Empire Mayring renamed *Lochbroom*
Empire Mayring, a sister ship to the *Empire Maysong*, was launched by Scott and Sons of Bowling in 1946 and then lay in Bowling Harbour in an uncompleted state until purchased by David MacBrayne Ltd. in March

1947. She was taken to Ardrossan Dockyard Ltd where a five-cylinder British Polar diesel engine was fitted and the bridge and all accommodation was relocated aft. With the forward bridge and deckhouse, as shown on the photographs of *Empire Mayring,* removed, a single mast with derricks fore and aft was fitted to serve two hatches.

This was a very fortuitous purchase as the MacBrayne cargo services demanded shelter deck type ships for cattle and parcel type cargo rather than maximum deadweight and the *Empire May-* types were unique in being such small ships of the shelter deck type. As *Lochbroom* she served on various West Highland routes until sold in July 1971.

Loch Frisa photographed by Dan McDonald at Lancefield Quay, Glasgow on 26th June 1949. *[J. and M. Clarkson collection]*

Ottawa Maycliff (built in Canada) and renamed *Loch Frisa*
Not content with buying one ship of the above type, in 1949 a MacBrayne senior master took delivery of this ship, then named *Marleen,* at Rotterdam and brought her back to Irvine (via Dublin with a Coast Lines cargo) for conversion in a similar fashion to *Empire Mayring* although in her case the steam machinery was retained. *Loch Frisa* spent her latter years as spare and relief vessel and was sold in July 1963.
IAN RAMSAY, Garmoyle, Main Road, Langbank, Renfrewshire PA14 6XP

Rakaia revisited
I find all 37 Ships in Focus 'Records' interesting and informative. Of particular interest to me in issue 37 are the two photographs and text on page 41 of the *Whakatane* and the *Essex* and also the letter on page 58 about the sail-assisted Atlantic crossing of the *Rakaia.* There may well have been problems with fresh water on that passage, but for the chief steward to run short of eggs and bacon on a cadet ship is unthinkable! It was in Captain Lawson's nature to be polite, even when administering a 'dressing down'. I had the pleasure to serve in the *Remuera* (ex *Parthia*) under his command in 1962 and 1963. He was regarded throughout the New Zealand Shipping Co. Ltd. as a true gentleman.
BARRY PARSONS by e-mail

Manchester matters
I pick up 'Record' 37 and it falls open at pages 4/5. The sight of the once-familiar turrets of the African Oil Mills immediately powers up lapsed memory circuits. Press on and, although it pains me as a scouser of fifty years' provenance to admit it, all those marvellously atmospheric shots of the Manchester Ship Canal reopen acres of previously idle brain storage once again.

For instance, going up the 'cut' on Paddy Henderson's *Kabala* on the first day of 1966 with the tugs attending our progress in relays and us waving to the Bank Holiday pedestrians as we passed through the Warrington swing bridges. What did they make of our decks piled high with logs from West Africa? Coming down the way a decade later on Harrison's *Plainsman* dead ship following a disastrous cargo fire. It was always a bit of an adventure tackling the Canal with T. and J. Harrisons' ships. The run crowd rarely made it away from the pub up the road from Dock Number 8, so the Manchester riggers had to stay on to see us down the Canal. A few stragglers made it to Mode Wheel but most missed their chance and then enjoyed a punch-up with the substitutes that had been engaged from the Liverpool 'pool' to replace them at Eastham Lock. Your photographers naturally chose sunny days but fog was a winter hazard, spending a whole day on one transit tied up at Runcorn Old Quay whilst the crew totted up 'loss of sleep' and 'recurring loss of sleep' payments. But it was the bridges that caused the most heartache, the mate who loaded the ship in from the Gulf of Mexico rarely had to live with the trim consequences on leaving Manchester. On one occasion, with Harrison's *Philosopher*, we passed all the test wires bar the last and the pilot and his helmsman had the tricky task of holding us in the short lagoon between Latchford Lock and the railway viaduct whilst Chippy and I used a trusty seven-pound maul to beat flat the guardrail atop the after mast. The test wire must have been at fault because we then cleared the viaduct with more than a fathom of headway. Happy days? Maybe. Boring? Never. Keep up the good work.
JOHN GOBLE, 55 Shanklin Road, Southampton SO15 7RG

Just a couple of inaccuracies in your otherwise excellent article featuring the Manchester Ship Canal. Firstly, you state the *Greenport* was laid up for a while at Latchford. The dolphins at Latchford were never used for that purpose, only for vessels which were waiting for other vessels to pass or their air draft was too high for the gauge wire. Secondly, you state the *MSC Archer* was sold to the Maltese in 1970 when on page 54 it is shown waiting to be demolished at Dalmuir. It was the *MSC Arrow* that was sold to the Maltese after she had been converted to diesel.
COLIN LEONARD, 60 Halton Road, Runcorn, Cheshire WA7 5SB
Thanks to Reg Bailey for also pointing out our embarrassing confusion of tugs. Ed.

I was delighted to see a large portion of 'Record' 37 devoted to the Manchester Ship Canal - a now much under used waterway. Having now retired from the company after 32 years, it gives me more time to research its fascinating history. Therefore I feel the need to put the record straight on a number of matters.

83

The article on British and Continental Steamship Co. Ltd. shows a crane at the bottom of Number 6 Dock, Salford in 1935. This is not the 1937-built *The 250 Ton Crane* but its predecessor *Titan*. It had a fixed jib with a vertical lifting stem at its tip. I believe the hull comprised of a series of pontoons built on the River Weaver. I would welcome any information regarding this craft as little appears to be known as to its origins: most MSC craft do not appear in 'Lloyd's Register'.

'Dredging in the Port of Manchester' omitted the pontoon bucket dredgers *Irwell* (1) and *Mersey* also built 1890 by Fleming and Ferguson, Paisley. The former operated in the Salford/Pomona Docks until the late 1940s. One of these is depicted behind the tug *Florida* on page 45. Numerous other dredgers operated for the MSC in their early days but no doubt type space limits their inclusion. The *MSC Dart* was not in fact a 'D' class dredging tug but a launch/workboat.
REG BAILEY, 7 Cressbrook Road, Stockton Heath, Warrington WA4 6JH

Manchester Liners and Prince Line did not form a joint Mediterranean service with conventional ships (as is the inference on page 27 of 'Record' 37) but did institute a joint container service from 1971 using chartered vessels until appropriate container tonnage could be constructed. For at least 75 years previously, Prince Line had run a conventional Mediterranean break-bulk service both before and after the Furness purchase in 1916. At least post-Second World War, the service was based at Number 6 Shed, Number 7 Dock, Salford using smaller, three-hatch, Burntisland vessels starting with *Maltese Prince* of 1946 and at Canary Wharf, West India Dock using the larger, four-hatch vessels. The trade was further complicated by the Arab League's Jewish boycott. It would perhaps have been more accurate to say that the Prince Line conventional service to the Mediterranean was run in conjunction with the Johnston Warren Lines' Eastern Mediterranean and Black Sea services with some of the latter's ships (actually sisters of the Prince Line vessels) such as *Beechmore* and *Pinemore* going on to the Prince Line berth when the Great Lakes were closed to navigation during the winter months. This was prior to the ships being renamed *English Prince* and *African Prince* in 1965.

The *Black Prince* photograph is a bit of a curiosity showing as it does a London ship in the Manchester Ship Canal. Certainly the hull colour dates the photo to the late 1950s or early 1960s before a lighter colour was introduced to this part of the Furness fleet.
GEORGE SWAINE, Rectory Cottage, Streat, East Sussex BN6 8RX

Beechmore (top) was renamed *English Prince* in 1965. *[Top: J. and M. Clarkson collection, bottom: Ships in Focus]*

Greek additions and amendments

I found the 'British Yard, Greek Tramp - Revisited' very interesting and touching when I saw a lot of ships owned by Chian owners, many of them registered at Chios and not Piraeus as usual, and I was thinking of how many generations of my compatriots have sailed on board them. Of special interest were the Doxford cargo liners owned by Fafalios and Lyras, such as the *Finax* (page 235). The author omitted another sister, the *Atalanti* of George Livanos (the firm I sailed with as radio officer). A handsome ship, as was the whole class, her accommodation was considered spartan by the crews compared with contemporary Japanese-built bulkers of the company, e.g. having fans instead of air conditioning. Due to their speed and cargo gear, all these ships were usually chartered to well-known liner companies and in the era of containerisation they served places with limited port facilities.
EVANGELOS TZARDIS, Calypsous 15, GR-185 39, Piraeus, Greece

Grovelling apologies are due to Michael Matantos, who wrote a most interesting letter about Greek ships built in Britain and which was published on page 57 of 'Record' 37. Midway through the second paragraph we referred to a Dr. J. Ramsay Geddie, when Mr Matantos clearly wrote about a Dr. J. Ramsay Gebbie. This was a misguided effort on the part of the editor to correct what sounded an unlikely name.

RECORD REVIEWS

A THICKET OF BUSINESS: A HISTORY OF THE BOWRING FAMILY AND THE BOWRING GROUP OF COMPANIES by Peter Bowring
283-page hardback published by The Memoir Club at £19.95

Although two earlier histories of Bowring exist (published in 1940 and 1962), the company is not generally as well known to shipping historians as its size and longevity should merit. Between its foundation in 1818 and its takeover and final exit from shipping in the early 1980s, Bowring owned or managed well over 200 vessels. A new history is therefore welcome, and there can be no doubt that this one adds significantly to our knowledge of what became one of the most diversified of Britain's major maritime ventures. Although the author admits to having depended heavily on the existing literature, his book is particularly valuable, not only because it completes the history of the business up to its takeover in 1980, but also due to the fact that it has been written by a member of its founding family. Most of the company's pre-Second World War records were destroyed in the Luftwaffe's assault on the Liverpool dock area in 1941, and personal insights into the management of what was very much a family business (which did not seek a public listing until 1965) provide at least a partial substitute for their loss.

The Bowring business was built up in the early decades of the 19th century on the rather fragile foundations of trade with Newfoundland, one of the more marginal of Britain's overseas possessions. By the middle of Queen Victoria's reign it had grown into both a significant ship owner and one of the largest commercial ventures in St John's. It continued to diversify thereafter, not least in the shipping field as one of the pioneers of the oil tanker trade, and a major player in marine insurance. An indication of the range of just the shipping arm can be taken from a pair of vessels launched in 1909-1911 which were designed to operate as passenger liners in the nascent US cruise trade for most of the year, but could be converted to sealers during the hunting season! Ultimately insurance and other financial services interests overtook the shipping business in importance, but Bowring's last new vessel, the dry bulk carrier *Desdemona*, was launched as late as 1978, only two years before Bowring was taken over by the world's largest insurance broker, the US-based Marsh and McLennan.

The author writes in a clear and crisp style, and is admirably candid about the personalities and business performance of some of his ancestors. Beyond providing a detailed analysis of the Bowring family and its associates, he also demonstrates a clear grasp of the workings of the company's businesses. Ships and shipping operation are covered in some detail, and maritime historians are only likely to be able to fault him on the occasional error of detail, such as the unintentional shortening of the Liverpool ship-owners Rankin and Gilmour to Rank and Gilmour, or the identification of the German raider responsible for sinking the tanker *Cymbeline* in 1940 as the non-existent *Narvik* instead of the *Widder*.

It must be stressed, however, that this is very much a family business history and does not provide the sort of detailed ship coverage present in most specialist publications. While the history of some vessels is covered in considerable detail, and all the ships owned in the post-sail era are at least mentioned, there is no fleet list, and the very skimpy index covers only people and neither ships nor shipping companies. In addition, the otherwise excellent photographic sections include only a handful of ship pictures. Maritime business historians should certainly read this book, but it might not appeal to dedicated ship enthusiasts.

Malcolm Cooper

THE WINSTON SPECIALS, TROOPSHIPS VIA THE CAPE 1940-1943 by Archie Munro
510-page hardback published by Maritime Books, at £25.00

The author is a senior master mariner and a Fellow of the Institute of Navigation who writes clearly and with authority. His book is an accurate historical record of a campaign which was fought and emphatically won, partly because the enemy never fully realised that it was taking place.

In mid-1940 Germany was preparing to invade Britain from France and the Low Countries. Italy had joined Germany and shut the Mediterranean. Britain, instead of concentrating on self defence, decided to send the cream of her remaining forces 13,000 miles round the Cape to secure Egypt and the Middle East. Such a scheme was only possible because in 1940 Britain and the Dominions controlled half of the world's passenger ships.

This book is the history of the WS convoys, the Winston Specials which carried over one million British and allied personnel eastwards from 1940 to 1943. The contents cover pre-war trooping, early troop moves from the United Kingdom, and Dominions, and the loss of Europe to the Nazis in 1939-1940. There follow 18 chapters giving the detailed history of 52 separate WS convoys. There are extensive chapter notes and seven appendices including personnel embarked in the United Kingdom, ports of embarkation, lists of troopships, and maps showing convoy routes. Finally the index, or rather indices, list separately Allied warships, Axis warships, troopships (over 200 of them), other merchant ships, military formations and units, and individual personnel. Instead of giving endless page numbers, the index gives the convoy number or numbers relevant to each ship or unit. The system works well.

The amount of research undertaken by the author is formidable, including the movement cards maintained by the Ministry of War Transport for each ship, Admiralty records, war diaries, company histories, masters' reports, Clyde Navigation records, and regimental histories. He succeeds in making the reader feel he is alongside the convoy commodore as the voyage unfolds, with the additional advantage of having hindsight whenever that is helpful.

The return voyages, the SW convoys, sometimes unescorted, often included a visit to the Americas to load food and other essentials for home. At one time 130,000 Italian prisoners required transport. The last census revealed that two out of every seven inhabitants in the Bedford area have ethnic connections to Italy! Remembering how content many of the young Italian prisoners were to work on English farms, is it too far-fetched to attribute this to the SW convoys?

Of the 64 photographs, many of them not previously published, 42 may be described as wartime ship portraits, fascinating pictures of these famous old ships, some with boats swung out, with numerous gun tubs, paravane gear, life-rafts and wind sails rigged to ventilate troop decks. Sadly in my copy of the book eleven of the ships have their extremities either removed by the guillotine, or disappearing into the binding.

This is an important book and no library covering warfare or maritime affairs should be without a copy. For the rest of us, anyone interested in war at sea or the history of passenger shipping will find it excellent value for money.

John V. Bartlett

BEACON HILL
Captain A.W. Kinghorn

Fares Reefer. [The late Alwyn McMillan/Ian J. Farquhar collection]

Singapore does not permit a ship to be registered there if she is more than 15 years old, so when in 1981 the Vestey organisation bought the 1965-built *Fares Reefer* from Fares (pronounced 'Farriz') Oceanic Shipping S.A.R.L. of Lebanon, they took the unusual step (for them) of re-registering her in Hong Kong - then still British.

Between the two world wars the Vestey family's principal shipping line, Blue Star, traded regularly to China where they loaded frozen eggs for one of Britain's leading confectionary manufacturers, but these ships were always based and registered in London. It was not until 1953 that they entered the Far East trade with a dedicated service from Singapore to Australia, setting up Austasia Line with offices in Anson Road.

A new company
The new company's first ship was the *Malay* of 4,300gt, which had been laid down at Pickersgill's Sunderland shipyard as Booth Line's *Clement*. Launched 4th October 1952 as the *Malay Star* she became simply *Malay* during her fitting out, when it was decided to form a new company rather than operate as part of Blue Star Line. Austasia Line continued until 1997, employing mainly ships transferred from the associated Booth Line on cargo liner trades between Singapore, Malaysian ports, New Guinea and Australia. When this new line was first set up, Singapore was still a British Crown Colony and the ships registered there wore the red ensign. With independence in 1965, the Austasia ships were re-registered in London.

However, several years later they reverted to carrying Singapore upon their sterns, wearing the Singapore merchant red ensign, as they continued to do until Austasia Line and its subsequent Merlion Shipping Agency finally closed its doors.

In 1980 it had been decided to operate further afield and two P&O ships were purchased, *Taupo* and *Tekoa*, renamed *Mandama* and *Mahsuri* respectively. These fine, traditional cargo liners with three hatches forward of the bridge and two abaft in what had become the classic manner, were built at Sunderland by Bartrams in 1966 for the New Zealand Shipping

The *Malay* later held the names *Mahsuri, Benedict, Renoir* and *Diamond Star* before being broken up in Taiwan in 1973. *[Lindsay Rex/Russel Priest]*

Taupo (top left) and *Tekoa* (top right) in P&O colours. They took the names *Mandama* (middle) and *Mahsuri* (bottom) respectively when bought by Austasia Line. *[Top left: Tom Rayner/Roy Fenton collection, top right: Keith Byass/Roy Fenton collection, middle and bottom: Russell Priest]*

Company. Not yet 14 years old they were still eligible for Singapore registry. Like all Austasia Line ships they were manned by mostly British Blue Star officers with Singapore Chinese petty officers and ratings.

A new trade

Iran had begun ordering frozen sheep meat from New Zealand in addition to mutton on the hoof shipped from Australia. Rachid Fares of Lebanon owned the livestock carriers *Farid Fares* (6,667/1950), *Persia* (8,752/1951) and *Danny F.* (22,386/1961, a former tanker); all managed by Common Brothers of Newcastle-on-Tyne with British officers and Indian crews. These ships loaded live sheep in Australia - Adelaide or, more often, Fremantle - where loading day echoed to the clip-clopping of horses' hooves and the crack of stock whips while the drovers and their dogs steered thousands of loudly bleating sheep into coralled walkways up to the ship amid rising clouds of dust. These animals were carried to the Islamic countries of the Middle East where they would be slaughtered according to Islamic law. Live mutton from New Zealand was also considered and even tried but when it was realised that the extra week at sea greatly increased mortality among the four-footed passengers, Iran decided to import her New Zealand mutton already slaughtered and frozen. Iranian mullahs travelled to attend at the New Zealand abattoirs, ensuring the animals were killed according to Islamic custom. So,

Farid Farez (top) was completed as the *Lions Gate* at Malmo, Sweden in 1950 for A.A. Johnson. Bought in 1973 she was converted at Singapore to carry live sheep. The *Persia* (bottom) was built at Trieste, Italy as the *Asia*. Bought and renamed in 1975 she was similarly converted in 1977 and survived until December 1985 when she arrived at Gadani Beach, Pakistan to be broken up. [Both: Russell Priest]

the export of New Zealand frozen lamb and mutton got under way and the 'new' *Mandama* and *Mahsuri* entered the trade: frozen meat to the Gulf, light ship back to New Zealand.

These two ships had been purchased directly from P&O's Strick Line. They became redundant when the parent company decided to place their faith entirely in container ships. Well maintained by Austasia Line in their smart livery of grey hulls and white superstructure, surmounted with black-topped white funnel emblazoned with the big black-encircled A, they were still handsome vessels. Third of this class to come on the market was the *Westmorland*, a product of Lithgows, Port Glasgow. Whereas her two sisters had passed within the P&O group from New Zealand Shipping to Federal Steam Navigation Company in 1969, thence to Strick Line in 1977 via P&O General Cargo Division, the *Westmorland* had been sold in 1980 to Rachid Enterprises of Australia, the Lebanese company which already owned the livestock carriers. Mr Fares was ruefully realising that even from Australia the long voyage up through the tropics took its toll and sheep mortality in the livestock carriers was regrettably high. Iran were now accepting frozen meat - so Mr Fares bought the *Westmorland*.

Naming her *Fares Reefer*, he had her painted white with green boot topping. The funnel in pillar box red with a white band was the Lebanese flag without the cedar tree. With his livestock carriers he placed her under Common Brothers' management. But profitability of this strictly one-way trade depended on a rapid turnround at the discharge port. When ships - even reefers which usually were given precedence - began to spend weeks, sometimes months, anchored in the Shatt Al Arab awaiting berths, *Fares Reefer*'s profit rapidly ebbed into loss and Mr Fares decided to stick with the (mostly) quick rather than the dead. The Vesteys, always interested in buying good refrigerated tonnage, snapped her up in 1981, to eventually rename her *Beacon Hill*.

New ship

Only when it was realised that she was now too old for Singapore registry was an entirely new company formed, the Dunston Shipping Company of Hong Kong. Her colour scheme was untouched save for the addition of 22 small black vertical rectangles painted along the white funnel band - eleven each side. With British officers and Singapore Chinese crew she proceeded to New Zealand where she loaded a full cargo of frozen lamb for Bandar Abbas, on the Iranian side of the Gulf, just inside the Straits of Hormuz. (These days the other Middle East nations call it the Arabian Gulf but to Iran it is still, of course, Persian.) When she put into Khor Fakkan,

Westmorland (top) in P&O colours, as *Fares Reefer* (middle) and as *Beacon Hill* (bottom) The latter two views clearly show the Hallen derricks. *[Top: Roy Fenton collection, middle: The late Alwyn McMillan/Ian J. Farquhar collection, bottom: author]*

just outside the Gulf, in October 1981 to change a few crew members, I joined her.

She lay offshore at anchor along with many other ships, mostly tankers which were awaiting orders off Khor Fakkan, ready at short notice to proceed wherever their owners or charterers directed. When the launch taking me out to the ship passed under *Beacon Hill*'s stern I saw that the flag hanging limp in the calm morning sunshine was a blue ensign. Had Captain Ian MacKillop (who I was to relieve) joined the Royal Naval Reserve? I soon discovered he had not - hidden in the blue flag's hanging folds was the badge of Her Majesty's Crown Colony of Hong Kong.

Expecting to weigh anchor at once and proceed to Bandar Abbas I received an urgent instruction to wait. Do

89

not weigh anchor (do not pass GO or collect £200). Remain on short notice to sail but, for the time being, proceed no further. It seemed my ship had become a floating cold store - a common enough practice down the years when shore storage space was unavailable. And the Khor Fakkan anchorage, in friendly waters during those troubled times, was strategically placed. This was soon after the Iranian revolution, the new regime had yet to be accepted as a responsible government and the situation in the Gulf was tense. For this reason the *Beacon Hill* was moved out of the anchorage where she was vulnerable into the safety of the port - an artificial harbour recently constructed to cater for large container vessels. It was during our move into port that I learned that Harbour Master Captain Jim Peattie who took us in was a former Clyde Pilot - before which he had been a captain in the New Zealand Shipping Company - my ship's first owners. Not only that, he had been her very first pilot, taking the new *Westmorland* down the Clyde from her Port Glasgow shipyard. During the following two months alongside I had plenty of time to study this ship - my employer's latest acquisition - in detail. Much of her refrigeration machinery and equipment was in poor condition but rapidly being brought up to scratch by our own engineers. Main engine was an 8-cylinder Sulzer 2SCSA - almost identical to that in the heavy lift ship *Australia Star* of which I had been chief officer in 1965/6 when the *Westmorland* was also new. I had in fact visited her in Gladstone Dock, Liverpool, in July 1966 at the invitation of her second officer who was an old friend. Proudly he showed me round his fine new vessel and I saw that both ships had the exterior steel decks around bridge and accommodation thickly coated with that bitumastic compound which had recently come into vogue. 'As used in the new *Oriana*' I had been told in the builders' yard. Planked wooden decks were going out of fashion. Beautiful as they are, they were becoming prohibitively expensive - and perhaps even in 1965 the environmentalists were applying pressure to leave the forests alone? But it was *Westmorland*'s cargo derricks which had my main interest. Hallen derricks were quite new to those of us who had spent our seafaring lives with cargo cranes or derricks rigged in union purchase. This was a rig dating from the sailing ships, where a yardarm would be plumbed over the quay and a midships block rigged over the hatch. The two cargo runners (wire ropes from the cargo winches) running through yardarm and midships blocks were shackled to a single hook. Cargo was discharged by hoisting the load vertically out of the hold until clear of the hatch coaming, then swinging it out on the yardarm runner to

The Dhow Waddi at Khor Fakkan (above) and the new port (below) with alongside (left to right) *Halifax Star,* the Swedish *Durian* on charter to Blue Star, and the *Beacon Hill. (Both: author)*

Beacon Hill. [Ted Drake/Russell Priest]

be lowered to the quay or barge alongside. Loading was, of course, the same operation in reverse. In our day, derricks in union purchase were still known as the 'yardarm derrick' and 'midships derrick' lifting, usually, no more than three tons per hoist. But here Mr Hallen had given us at each hatch a single swinging derrick with a safe working load of 20 tons, set up on a bipod mast whose prominent masthead rounded frames provided fitting points for the twin topping lifts and also prevented the derrick collapsing when swung outboard. A very handy rig - modern technology, sea style!

A thoughtfully designed ship, she had a walkway-gallery along the foreside of the wheelhouse to give access for cleaning salt spray off the windows. Accommodation was spacious and comfortable. The captain's lavishly furnished dayroom had a handsome open fireplace (ornamental only), a separate office and a large twin-bedded bedroom with en-suite bathroom - all situated on the foreside of the deck under the bridge.

Large steel watertight doors in the ship's sides port and starboard gave access to the engine room - most useful in port for taking bunkers, spare parts and stores. Straight raked stem and rounded cruiser stern gave her an elegant yet workmanlike appearance. Although I could not inspect the holds - full of frozen meat - I knew that her cargo-carrying spaces were lined with brown-varnished wood cladding over cork and glass wool insulation and that the dunnage on which the cargo was stowed consisted of wood pallets, scrubbed and then varnished. Refrigerated ships had for many years used vast quantities of new, clean timber as dunnage to ensure correct circulation of the cold air refrigerating the cargo. The general cargoes of machinery, unpacked cars, lorries and buses, steel and all manner of industrial, medical and domestic items carried outward from the UK and Europe to the Southern Dominions were dunnaged, shored off, tommed and secured with used timber, but every time you loaded a refrigerated cargo in Australia or New Zealand new timber had to be purchased. A hold making ready to carry frozen cargo was first thoroughly washed clean and dried, then laid with 3" x 3" pine bearers four feet apart in the direction of cold airflow, overlaid with 6" x 1" planks - which in a big ship with numerous 'tween decks took a lot of timber. In the halcyon days of full cargoes and high freights the cost of this dunnage - and wages paid to carpenters employed to sawcut and nail it all in position - was considered of no great importance. The Lloyd's surveyors in the loading ports required it anyway, before they would pass you for loading.

But by the 1980s the costs of break bulk cargo operations - as compared with containerisation - were coming under close scrutiny. Wages, fuel, stores and all costs were escalating while freight rates were at best remaining steady, if not falling. Increasingly, Economy with a capital E became the watchword and one way of drastically cutting dunnage bills was to use the versatile wooden pallet, trimmed to shape where necessary to fit the ship's holds' interior lines. Varnished (by the ship's crew) to make easily washable, and stowed out of the way when heavy, dirty general cargoes were carried, these 'dunnage-pallets' were a boon in the last days of the old refrigerated break-bulk cargo liners. This idea was introduced into Blue Star Line by cargo superintendent, the late Captain David Thomas, and *Beacon Hill* was the first ship in which I'd seen it used. It worked well.

Unloading at last

We stayed waiting for over two months in Khor Fakkan, an interesting little port which had been developed by the Arab ruler from a tiny fishing and coastwise haven to a container terminal of international importance. Hoping to spend New Year with our Scottish harbourmaster and his family - and most of the port's officials were also Scottish - I was instead ordered to sail for Bandar Abbas on 31st December. This only entailed a six hours run up through the Straits of Hormuz. On arrival I was directed by Port Control over the VHF telephone to anchor and await a berth. Two days later our pilot boarded and took us in, to an artificial harbour as yet far from completion. Harbour lights and buoys were not yet in place, more dredging was necessary (as we found when we slid in over a sandbank), while the quay

- when we eventually reached it - was unsurfaced brown dust - churned to instant mud after a shower of rain. Young soldiers of the Revolutionary Guard were in full control and paid us frequent unheralded visits to ensure we were not breaking any of the numerous laws recently instigated – such as thou shalt not drink alcohol nor play Western music on thy radios.

However, the cargo went out in fine style thanks to Mr Hallen's derricks and enthusiastic local winch drivers. The meat was loaded on the wharf into huge freezer lorries which would carry it over the mountains to Teheran, a return journey taking several days. I was the only member of our ship's company to be allowed ashore, and this only granted with hard won permission, to visit the agent in his house for an evening. He implored me, if any stowaways were found when we departed, please do not bring them back, as that would have grave consequences, probably the death penalty. I had experience of two Iranian stowaways in my previous ship - a pair who, fortunately, were allowed to leave the ship legally in our next port, Kuwait.

This time, however - no stowaways - and we returned to Khor Fakkan on 13th January 1982 to await orders. Our two Austasia Line sisters *Mandama* and *Mahsuri* also came in, having delivered meat cargoes at other Gulf ports. At that time the worldwide reefer trades were over tonnaged, and too many ships were chasing too few cargoes. Together we waited while Blue Star Line's Reefer Trading Division in Leadenhall Street, London, strove to fix us cargoes. January was traditionally a quiet time for reefer ships, in between seasons, and even in the palmy days it was not uncommon for a few ships from the big British reefer companies to lay up for a few weeks, usually in the Blackwater or the Fal.

After a couple of days the *Mandama* was ordered out, a cargo had been found for her. Next week we remaining two were also ordered out, to proceed to Fremantle at easy speed. By the time we arrived, it was hoped, cargoes would have been found.

Reduced to tramping
It will be realised by now that these fine cargo liners, built to maintain their owners' long established regular trades between Europe/UK and the Southern Dominions, were having to seek cargoes tramping, ousted by the new container ships, each of which could carry as much cargo as five of the older ships, and faster, with minimal time in port. History was repeating itself. Tramping was how the clipper ships ended their days when steam was beginning to take the cream of the cargoes.

On 6th February, by which time we were well across the Indian Ocean, position latitude 21 04 south, longitude 101 13 east, I was ordered to stop and drift, to save fuel. *Mahsuri*, ten miles ahead and making the same speed, was also stopped, and together we drifted. Some days she was completely in view on the horizon, on other days only her masts were visible, such are the vagaries of ocean currents. Then she was ordered to Brisbane and disappeared, leaving us to drift alone. By the time I was ordered to resume passage to Fremantle we were in latitude 17 36 south, longitude 95 09 east, having drifted back a distance of 421 miles along a 'course' of 301 degrees true, in ten days.

At Fremantle there was still no cargo for us - Captain MacKillop returned from his leave and I flew home. The ship carried on to New Zealand where, in Wellington, a new Singapore crew joined to replace those who had sailed with me and were now due voyage leave. *Beacon Hill* was to cross the South Pacific to Valparaiso, where she loaded fruit for the Gulf. By this time, however, Argentina had invaded the Falklands and the subsequent conflict made the Magellan Straits and adjacent waters a no-go area for merchant shipping.

Captain MacKillop therefore took her well south of Cape Horn, expecting to see few ships if any in those lonely waters. Visibility was poor, with mist and rain rendering the sighting of possible icebergs difficult, when suddenly a large ship's echo appeared astern on the *Beacon Hill*'s radar. Approaching at well over 20 knots, overtaking, this had to be an Argentine warship in search of prey, seeking to avenge the loss of their cruiser *General Belgrano*! Then, out of the ether crackled a message on the VHF. '*Beacon Hill, Beacon Hill* this is *ACT 7*. How the devil are you Ian?' *ACT 7* (1977/44,000) was a large Blue Star-managed container ship - commanded by Ian MacKillop's brother Don. Not often you meet your brother off Cape Horn these days!

Homeward bound from Port Chalmers at 22 knots, *ACT 7* rapidly disappeared into the murk ahead, leaving *Beacon Hill* to continue her precarious trading until July 1984, when she was laid up in the Dubai port of Jebel Ali. By 1985 it was realised that the 20-year-old ship had no future. The Iranian meat contracts had expired, no other trades opened up, and she was sold to China for scrap, arriving in the Huanpu River, Shanghai, on 6th March 1985. Her two sisters, *Mandama* and *Mahsuri*, had gone for scrap at Kaohsiung the previous year.

The only other Dunston Shipping Company vessel was the *Crest Hill*, ex *Timaru Star* (1967/8,366), transferred from Blue Star Line in 1983. She preceded *Beacon Hill*'s arrival in a Chinese scrap yard by five days in 1985. These ships were indeed the last of an era of traditional cargo liners, splendid vessels which had, for many years, formed a major part of the backbone of the British Merchant Navy.

Don MacKillop's ship, the *ACT 7*. [J. and M. Clarkson]

THE RISE AND FALL OF BLACK STAR LINE
Peter Newall

On 6th March 1957 Ghana gained its independence after almost 140 years of British rule. The former Gold Coast colony was the first democratic independent state in sub-Saharan colonial Africa and was soon followed by numerous new African states, including Nigeria in 1960.

Ghana's first president was Dr. Kwame Nkrumah (1909-1972) who had a grand vision of a united Africa liberated from colonial rule. Educated in the United States, Dr. Nkrumah was inspired by the ideas of the Jamaican Marcus Garvey who promoted a 'Back to Africa' movement among Afro-Americans in the 1910s and 1920s. Garvey was also keen to see black Americans more involved in the business community and in 1919 he established the Black Star Steamship Corporation or Black Star Line as it became more commonly known. It was hoped that the new company would transport goods produced by black businesses in the Caribbean, North America and Africa. *Yarmouth* (1887/1,452), a former Canadian Pacific Railway's passenger ferry, was purchased but, although she made a few trips to the Caribbean with an all-black crew, the service was not a success. By the time Black Star Line bought *Orion* (1902/6,026, formerly HAPAG's *Prinz Oskar*) in 1922 the company was in serious financial difficulties through mismanagement and a series of self-inflicted crises. It folded soon after Marcus Garvey was indicted for mail fraud in February 1922.

Until 1957 the West Africa-UK trade was dominated by three British lines: Elder Dempster Line (with 64% of the Conference Lines cargo allocation), Palm Line (28.5%) and Guinea Gulf Line (7.5%). With the advent of independence, the government of Nigeria had discussions with neighbouring countries about establishing a joint national shipping company. However, Ghana was determined to manage its own affairs and in September 1957 Black Star Line Ltd. was established with initial funds of £500,000. Given Dr. Nkrumah's association with Marcus Garvey, the company name may have been chosen in honour of the failed enterprise of the 1920s although the five-pointed black star is at the centre of the Ghanaian national flag.

President Nkrumah was also keen to break with the colonial past and, despite an offer of assistance from Elder Dempster Line, the Zim Israel Navigation Co. Ltd. of Haifa was appointed manager of the new line. Zim not only provided office and shore-side management, deck and engineering officers, it also subscribed 40% of the capital. The rest was provided by the state of Ghana. On the other hand, the Nigerian National Shipping Line founded in 1959 had Elder Dempster and Palm Line taking a 49% financial stake.

In October 1957 Black Star Line purchased its first ship *Marsdale* (1939/4,890) from the British firm Kaye, Son and Co. Ltd. In November Black Star became a full member of the West African Conference and was given the rights to operate a monthly service between West Africa and the UK with four ships. This it did with *Volta River* (ex *Marsdale*) and three Zim Line chartered motorships: *Galila* (1955/3,155) and the sisters *Dagan* (1954/5,099) and *Tappuz* (1954/5,099). The following year three more second-hand vessels were bought including a pair of 1943-built motor ships from The Hain Steam Ship Co. Ltd., *Trewidden* and *Trevince*, which were renamed *Ankobra River* and *Densu River* respectively. The third ship, *Hadar*, came from Zim Line and was renamed *Tano River*.

In the early years of independence, Ghanaian confidence was such that it invested heavily in industrial development, including a huge hydroelectric power plant on the Volta River and the building of a large new harbour at Tema, which replaced the anchorage at Accra. Black Star Line was also making a profit and in August 1960 the state became the sole owner when it purchased Zim Line's share of the company. Despite this change, Zim continued to be the managing agent for the company. It also provided technical support for the next stage of the company's development, an ambitious new building programme. In January 1960 an order worth £9 million was placed with the Dutch shipyard 'De Schelde',

The company's first ship, the *Volta River*, with black hull. *[J. and M. Clarkson]*

Pra River. [Newall Dunn collection]

Flushing for eight 7,500gt cargo-passenger motor ships to be delivered between 1961 and 1963 (two were subcontracted to a German yard at Lübeck). These ships would enable Black Star to provide regular cargo-passenger services from Ghana not only to the UK but also to North America, Northern Europe and the Mediterranean. Handsome shelter-deck ships, they were designed to carry general cargo including logs on the upper decks. Four were provided with reefer space whilst the remainder had deep tanks for the storage of vegetable oil. They also carried 12 passengers in comfortable accommodation. The first to be completed was *Pra River* in May 1961.

Shortly after the delivery in March 1963 of *Lake Bosomtwe*, the eighth and final ship from Holland, Black Star Line placed its first order with a British yard for four similar ships but with more powerful Sulzer-type engines. Thanks to a British government loan, *Sakumo Lagoon*, *Korle Lagoon* and *Benya River* were built on the Tyne in 1964 and 1965 by Swan Hunter and Wigham Richardson whilst *Nakwa River* was constructed in Glasgow by Barclay Curle, then part of the Swan Hunter Group. *Nakwa River* also differed from the other three ships in that she was fitted out as a 24-cadet training ship.

The final ship in the quartet, *Benya River*, had her passenger accommodation replaced by a special presidential suite for President Nkrumah, complete with office, entrance hall and illuminated cabinets for the display of ceremonial regalia. Dr. Nkrumah was now Life President in charge of a one-party state. His grand vision for Ghana had also plunged the country into immense debt. In a relatively short period Ghana had moved from being one of the richest countries in Africa to one of the poorest. By 1966 the country had enough of its great leader and not long after the official opening of the Volta Dam, he was overthrown and sent into exile.

Meanwhile, two more ships were constructed in Japan and, later in the decade, a final pair was built in Spain, bringing to a total 16 near-identical new ships arriving between 1961 and 1969. In 1968 Black Star and Zim mutually agreed to terminate Zim's managing agency of the line although Zim continued to give technical advice and remained the company's agent.

Sakumo Lagoon. [Newall Dunn collection]

Benya River. [Newall Dunn collection]

Throughout the 1970s, as Ghana lurched from crisis to crisis, so did the heavily indebted Black Star Line. Corruption was rife and the state-run company was forced to carry all cocoa exports at an operating loss. The ships were also delayed by problems delivering cocoa beans to Ghanaian ports.

In 1980 Black Star Line took delivery of four 13,000gt Korean-built multi-purpose cargo liners, which also had a 200 TEU container capacity. Near-identical ships with Stülcken-type derricks were built at the same yard for the Nigerian National Shipping Line. In the same year, Black Star was hit by a lengthy ship officers' strike. The fleet also suffered from lack of maintenance and ships were arrested for non-payment of debts. Because of the knock-on impact on Ghana's exports, the President of Ghana took charge and the Black Star top management was replaced by four West German advisors from the Hamburg-based company Marine Transport Consultants International. The government also agreed to take over the company's debts. However, after a relatively short time, the German team gave up and in April 1982 withdrew from the management agreement. Ships continued to be impounded or laid up and between 1983 and 1985 11 of the 1960s-built fleet were sold for scrap, mainly in Spain. By 1987 the sole ships in the fleet were the four seven-year-old multi-purpose vessels. The company struggled on with these ships into the 1990s and in 1998 *Keta Lagoon* and *Volta River* were sold, bringing to an end an interesting chapter in the development of shipping in Africa. It was also appropriate that Black Star Line started and ended its 41-year history with a ship called *Volta River*.

Tano River, one of the last class of four ships. [Newall Dunn collection]

FLEET LIST

1. VOLTA RIVER (1) 1957-1965
O.N. 167422 4,890g 2,963n
420.3 x 56.9 x 24.3 feet.
T.3-cyl. by North Eastern Marine Engineering Co. (1938) Ltd., Newcastle-on-Tyne.
13.12.1939: Launched by Lithgows Ltd., Port Glasgow (Yard No. 923) for The 'K' Steam Ship Co. Ltd. (Kaye, Son and Co. Ltd., managers), London as MARSDALE.
4.1940: Completed.
10.1957: Acquired by Black Star Line Ltd., Accra and renamed VOLTA RIVER.
1965: Sold to Psara Shipping Co., Monrovia, Liberia (G.C. Calafatis and Co. Ltd., Piraeus, Greece) and renamed PSARA
24.5.1967: Arrived at La Spezia for demolition by Lotti S.p.A.

2. ANKOBRA RIVER 1959-1964
O.N. 168406 7,273g 4984n
442.9 o.l. x 56.5 x 35.5 feet.
3-cyl. 2SCSA oil engines by William Doxford and Sons Ltd., Sunderland.
23.10.1942: Launched by William Doxford and Sons Ltd., Sunderland (Yard No. 699) for J. and C. Harrison Ltd., London as HARLESDEN.
3.1943: Completed.
1944: Sold to The Hain Steam Ship Co. Ltd., London.
1945: Renamed TREWIDDEN.
20.4.1959: Acquired by Black Star Line Ltd., Accra and renamed ANKOBRA RIVER.
1964: Sold to Tenes Shipping Co. S.A., Panama (G.C. Calafatis and Co. Ltd., Piraeus, Greece) and renamed ELAND under the Liberian flag.
1968: Sold to Tien Cheng Steel Manufacturing Ltd. for demolition.
29.10.68: Arrived at Kaohsiung

3. DENSU RIVER 1959-1967
O.N. 169571 7,292g 4,969n
428.8 o.l. x 56.5 x 35.5 feet.

Top: *Volta River* now with a grey hull. *[Newall Dunn collection]*
Middle: *Ankobra River. [Roy Fenton collection]*
Bottom: *Densu River. [Roy Fenton collection]*

3-cyl 2SCSA oil engines by William Doxford and Sons Ltd., Sunderland.
4.5.1943: Launched by William Doxford and Sons Ltd., Sunderland (Yard No. 705) for The Hain Steam Ship Co. Ltd., London as TREVINCE.
8.1943: Completed.
23.9.1959: Acquired by Black Star Line Ltd., Accra and renamed DENSU RIVER.
1967: Sold to Compania de Naviera Victoria S.A., Panama (Societa Armamento Marittimo in Nome Colletivo, Genoa, Italy) and renamed VICKY.

1973: Sold to Holivian Shipping Co. S.A., Panama.
4.6.1974: Arrived at Saigon under tow after engine had broken down during a voyage from Penang. Repairs were uneconomical and she was towed to Hong Kong.
27.7.1974: Arrived at Whampoa for demolition.

4. TANO RIVER (1) 1959-1966
2,574g 1,216n
330.6 x 46.11 x 19.1 feet.

T.3-cyl. by George Clark (1938) Ltd., Sunderland.
13.3.1949: Launched by Short Brothers Ltd., Sunderland (Yard No. 504) for Lama Compania de Vapores S.A., Panama (A.G. Pappadakis, Piraeus, Greece) as GEORGE.
7.1949: Completed.
1950: Sold to Zim Israel Navigation Co. Ltd., Haifa, Israel and renamed HADAR.
1959: Acquired by Black Star Line Ltd., Accra and renamed TANO RIVER.
1966: Sold to Arden Compania Naviera S.A., Panama (Pateras Brothers Ltd., Piraeus, Greece) and renamed ARDEN.
1969: Sold to Achaika Shipping Co. Ltd. S.A. (G. Tsitsilianis), Piraeus and renamed ACHAIKA HOPE.
8.12.1969: Wrecked on rocks off Razzoli Island, Northern Sardinia during a violent storm whilst on a voyage from Sete to Izmir in ballast. All crew were rescued.

5. PRA RIVER 1961-1981
7,351g 4,677n
460.11 x 60.3 x 23.3 feet.
5-cyl. 2SCSA Sulzer-type oil engines by N.V. Koninklijke 'De Schelde', Flushing, Holland; 4,500 BHP, 15 knots.
21.1.1961: Launched by N.V. Koninklijke 'De Schelde', Flushing, Holland (Yard No. 311) for Black Star Line Ltd., Accra as PRA RIVER.
13.5.1961: Completed.
1981: Sold to Notos Shipping Co. (Cortado Maritime Inc. (John Yannios)), Piraeus, Greece and renamed NOTOS.
1983: Sold to Chinese Compania Maritima S.A., Panama and renamed MAYON II.
26.7.83: Ran aground near Dakar in position 14.46 north by 17.32 west whilst on a voyage from Las Palmas to Lagos with a cargo of cement. In early 1984 the Senegalese Government had the wreck towed to deep water and scuttled.

6. OTCHI RIVER 1961-1984
7,378g 4,675n
460.11 x 60.4 x 23.3 feet.
5-cyl. 2SCSA Sulzer-type oil engines by N.V. Koninklijke 'De Schelde', Flushing, Holland; 4,500 BHP, 15 knots.
10.5.1961: Launched by Orenstein-Koppel and Lübecker Maschinenbau-Gesellschaft, Lübeck, West Germany (Yard No. 568) for Black Star Line Ltd., Accra as OTCHI RIVER.
11.1961: Completed.
6.8.1982-5.2.1984: Laid up at Takoradi.
1984: Sold to Desguaces Heme S.A, Gijon.
12.3.1984: Arrived Gijon under tow.
2.4.1984: Breaking up began.

7. OFFIN RIVER 1961-1983
7,354g 4,661n
460.11 x 60.3 x 23.3 feet.
5-cyl. 2SCSA Sulzer-type oil engines by N.V. Koninklijke 'De Schelde', Flushing, Holland; 4,500 BHP, 15 knots.
13.5.1961: Launched by N.V. Koninklijke 'De Schelde', Flushing, Holland (Yard No. 312) for Black Star Line Ltd., Accra as OFFIN RIVER.
9.1961: Completed.
6.10.1981-19.9.1983: Laid up under arrest at Avonmouth.
25.9.1983: Arrived at Aviles under tow from Avonmouth having been sold by creditors to Desguaces y Salvamentos S.A.
26.9.1983: Work began.

Tano River, formerly Zim Israel's Hadar. [Newall Dunn collection]

Otchi River. [Newall Dunn collection]

Offin River. [J. and M. Clarkson]

8. NASIA RIVER 1962-1984
7,390g 4,865n
460.11 x 60.4 x 23.3 feet.
5-cyl. 2SCSA Sulzer-type oil engines by N.V. Koninklijke 'De Schelde', Flushing, Holland; 4,500 BHP, 15 knots.
311.1.1962: Launched by Orenstein-Koppel and Lübecker Maschinenbau-Gesellschaft, Lübeck, West Germany (Yard No. 569) for Black Star Line Ltd., Accra as NASIA RIVER.
5.1962: Completed.
2.3.1980-16.2.1984: Laid up at Tema.
1984: Sold to Desguaces y Salvamentos, Spain.
3.4.1984: Arrived at Aviles under tow for breaking up.
14.4.1984: Work began.

Birim River. [Roy Fenton collection]

9. BIRIM RIVER 1962-1984
7,354g 4,661n
460.11 x 60.3 x 23.3 feet.
5-cyl. 2SCSA Sulzer-type oil engines by N.V. Koninklijke 'De Schelde', Flushing, Holland; 4,500 BHP, 15 knots.
30.9.1961: Launched by N.V. Koninklijke 'De Schelde', Flushing, Holland (Yard No. 313) for Black Star Line Ltd., Accra as AFRAM RIVER.
3.1962: Completed.
30.4.1980-16.2.1984: Laid up at Tema.
1984: Sold to Miguel Martins Pereira, Vigo.
30.3.1984: Arrived at Vigo under tow.
5.4.1984: Breaking up began.

10. AFRAM RIVER 1962-1983
7,356g 4,670n
460.11 x 60.3 x 23.3 feet.
5-cyl. 2SCSA Sulzer-type oil engines by N.V. Koninklijke 'De Schelde', Flushing, Holland; 4,500 BHP, 15 knots.
10.3.1962: Launched by N.V. Koninklijke 'De Schelde', Flushing, Holland (Yard No. 314) for Black Star Line Ltd., Accra as AFRAM RIVER.
9.1962: Completed.
29.6.1982-4.12.1983: Laid up at Takoradi.
1983: Sold to Desguaces y Salvamentos S.A.
6.1.1984: Arrived Aviles under tow for breaking up.
11.1.1984: Breaking up began.

11. KULPAWN RIVER 1962-1983
7,356g 4,670n
460.11 x 60.3 x 23.3 feet.
5-cyl. 2SCSA Sulzer-type oil engines by N.V. Koninklijke 'De Schelde', Flushing, Holland; 4,500 BHP, 15 knots.
9.6.1962: Launched by N.V. Koninklijke 'De Schelde', Flushing, Holland (Yard No. 315) for Black Star Line Ltd., Accra as KULPAWN RIVER.
11.1962: Completed.
14.11.1981-21.9.1983: Laid up under arrest at Avonmouth.

Kulpawn River. [J. and M. Clarkson]

26.9.1983: Arrived at Vigo under tow from Avonmouth having been sold by creditors to Gomez Jose Oliveira.
14.12.1983: Breaking up began.

12. LAKE BOSOMTWE 1963-1981
7,356g 4,670n
460.11 x 60.3 x 23.3 feet.
5-cyl. 2SCSA Sulzer-type oil engines by N.V. Koninklijke 'De Schelde', Flushing, Holland; 4,500 BHP, 15 knots.
24.11.1962: Launched by N.V. Koninklijke 'De Schelde', Flushing, Holland (Yard No. 316) for Black Star Line Ltd., Accra as LAKE BOSOMTWE.
3.1963: Completed.
1981: Sold to Dundrum Shipping Co. Ltd. (Transmed Shipping Ltd.), Limassol, Cyprus and renamed CHARMYL.
1.3.1985: Arrived Shanghai for demolition.

13. SAKUMO LAGOON 1964-1984
7,337g 4,234n
454.4 x 62.8 x 23.11 feet.
6-cyl. 2SCSA Sulzer-type oil engines by Wallsend Slipway and Engineering Co. Ltd., Wallsend; 7,200 BHP, 17 knots.
29.1.1964: Launched by Swan Hunter and Wigham Richardson Ltd., Wallsend (Yard No. 2005) for Black Star Line Ltd., Accra as SAKUMO LAGOON.
5.1964: Completed.
11.6.1983-4.4.1984: Laid up at Takoradi.
5.5.1984: Ran aground off Forcade Point near Aviles after tow broke whilst under tow by the Spanish tug AZNAR JOSE LUIS from Takoradi to breakers at Aviles. Wreck abandoned.

14. KORLE LAGOON 1964-1984
7,337g 4,243n
454.4 x 62.8 x 23.11 feet.
6-cyl. 2SCSA Sulzer-type oil engines by Wallsend Slipway and Engineering Co. Ltd., Wallsend; 7,200 BHP.
13.5.1964: Launched by Swan Hunter and Wigham Richardson Ltd., Wallsend (Yard No. 2006) for Black Star Line Ltd., Accra as KORLE LAGOON.
9.1964: Completed.
4.5.1983-14.9.1984: Laid up under arrest at Amsterdam.

Sakumo Lagoon. [Newall Dunn collection]

1984: Sold to Desguaces y Salvamentos S.A.
21.9.1984: Arrived at Aviles under tow from Amsterdam.
26.9.1984: Breaking up began.

15. OTI RIVER 1964-1984
7,478g 4,320n
455.0 x 62.8 x 23.11 feet.
6-cyl. 2SCSA Sulzer-type oil engines by Maizuru Shipbuilding and Engineering Co. Ltd., Maizuru, Japan.
4.1964: Launched by Hitachi Zosen, Osaka, Japan (Yard No. 4023) for Black Star Line Ltd., Accra as OTI RIVER.
9.1964: Completed.
2.4.1982-17.4.1984: Laid up under arrest at Hamburg.
1984: Sold to Desbar S.A.
24.4.1984: Arrived at Santander under tow from Hamburg.
5.7.1984: Breaking up began.

16. BIA RIVER 1965-1987
7,479g 4,319n
455.0 x 62.8 x 23.11 feet.
6-cyl. 2SCSA Sulzer-type oil engines by Uraga Heavy Industries Ltd., Yokosuka, Japan; 7,200 BHP.
12.1964: Launched by Uraga Heavy Industries Ltd., Yokosuka, Japan (Yard No. 851) for Black Star Line Ltd., Accra as BIA RIVER.
3.1965: Completed.
26.12.1987: Arrived at Gadani Beach to be broken up by Inter-Ocean Traders.
27.12.1987: Work began.

17. BENYA RIVER 1965-1985
7,337g 4,238n
454.6 x 62.8 x 23.11 feet.
6-cyl. 2SCSA Sulzer-type oil engines by Wallsend Slipway and Engineering Co., Wallsend; 7,200 BHP, 17 knots.
27.9.1965: Launched by Swan Hunter and Wigham Richardson Ltd., Wallsend (Yard No. 2008) for Black Star Line Ltd., Accra as BENYA RIVER.
11.1965: Completed.

Bia River. [Roy Fenton collection]

3.1985: Sold to Alice Co. Garment and Knitters Ltd., Accra, Ghana and renamed WATER WEALTH.
1985: Renamed JAH.
1987: Name reverted to WATER WEALTH.
30.11.1988: Arrived at Alang for demolition by Haryana Steel Co.

18. NAKWA RIVER 1965-1984
7,323g 3,899n
454.6 x 62.8 x 23.11 feet.
6-cyl. 2SCSA Sulzer-type oil engines by Wallsend Slipway and Engineering Co. Ltd., Wallsend; 7,200 BHP, 17 knots.
15.1.1965: Launched by Barclay Curle and Co. Ltd., Glasgow (Yard No. 752) for Black Star Line Ltd., Accra as NAKWA RIVER.
5.1965: Completed.
4.2.1982-4.4.1984: Laid up under arrest at Hamburg.
1984: Sold to Desbar S.A.
10.4.1984: Arrived at Santander under tow from Hamburg.
27.4.1984: Breaking up began.

19. SUBIN RIVER 1969-1987
7,155g 4,010n
455 x 62.8 x 23.11 feet.
6-cyl. 2SCSA oil engines by Sociedad Española de Construccion Naval; 7,200 BHP, 17 knots.
26.8.1968: Launched by Sociedad Española de Construccion Naval, Cadiz, Spain (Yard No. 144) for Black Star Line Ltd., Accra as SUBIN RIVER.
7.1969: Completed.
2.1987: Sold to Marine Eagle S.A., St Vincent, renamed MILOS F and resold to Indian shipbreakers.
4.1987: Arrived at Sachana for demolition by Mansoor Taherbhai.

20. KLORTE LAGOON 1969-1987
7.155g 4,010n
455.0 x 62.8 x 23.11 feet.
6-cyl. 2SCSA oil engines by Sociedad Española de Construccion Naval; 7,200 BHP, 17 knots.
18.1.1969: Launched by Sociedad Española de Construccion Naval, Cadiz, Spain (Yard No. 145) for Black Star Line Ltd., Accra as KLORTE LAGOON.
9.1969: Completed.
1.1987: Sold to Interspirit Maritime Co. Ltd., St Vincent, renamed MILOS E and resold to Indian shipbreakers.
26.4.1987: Arrived at Alang for demolition by Gupta Steel.

21. VOLTA RIVER (2) 1980-1998
13,004g 7,506n
167.3 (oa) x 22.92 x 9.79 metres.
6-cyl. 2SCSA oil engines by Mitsubishi Heavy Industries Ltd., Kobe, Japan; 14,400 BHP, 18 knots.
6.6.1979: Launched by Hyundai Heavy Industries Co. Ltd., Ulsan, South Korea (Yard No. 117) for Black Star Line Ltd., Accra as VOLTA RIVER.
3.1980: Completed.
1.1998: Sold to Altex Shipping Co. Ltd., Nicosia, Cyprus (Astron Maritime Company S.A., Athens, Greece) and renamed TOLEDO.

Above: *Nakwa River*. *[Newall Dunn collection]*
Below: *Klorte Lagoon*. *[FotoFlite]*
Bottom: *Klorte Lagoon* whilst on charter to D.A.L. *[FotoFlite]*

1999: Sold to Tafferel Shipping Co. Ltd., Cyprus (Pacific and Atlantic Corporation, Piraeus, Greece) and renamed EXPRESS HERCULES.
10.7.2002: Arrived at Mumbai for demolition.

22. TANO RIVER (2) 1980-1994
13,004g 7,506n
167.3 (oa) x 22.92 x 9.79 metres.
6-cyl. 2SCSA oil engines by Mitsubishi Heavy Industries Ltd., Kobe, Japan; 14,400 BHP, 18 knots.
15.8.1979: Launched by Hyundai Heavy Industries Co. Ltd., Ulsan, South Korea (Yard No. 118) for Black Star Line Ltd., Accra as TANO RIVER.
2.1980: Completed.
2.1994: Sold to Astron Maritime Company S.A., Piraeus and renamed VERANO under the Cyprus flag.
1999: Sold to Qualitas Shipping Co. Ltd., Cyprus (Pacific and Atlantic Corporation, Piraeus, Greece) and renamed EXPRESS HYPHESTOS.
14.6.2002: Arrived at Mumbai for demolition.

23. KETA LAGOON 1980-1998
13,004g 7,506n
167.3 (oa) x 22.92 x 9.79 metres.
6-cyl. 2SCSA oil engines by Mitsubishi Heavy Industries Ltd., Kobe, Japan; 14,400 BHP, 18 knots.
13.10.1979: Launched by Hyundai Heavy Industries Co. Ltd., Ulsan, South Korea (Yard No. 119) for Black Star Line Ltd., Accra as KETA LAGOON.
3.1980: Completed.
12.1980: Chartered to Andrew Weir and Co. Ltd., London and renamed TYNEBANK.
8.1981: Reverted to KETA LAGOON.
2.1998: Sold to Medog Shipping Co. Ltd., Nicosia, Cyprus (Astron Maritime Company S.A., Athens, Greece) and renamed ILION.
11.1998: Sold to Brentwood Commercial Corporation, Panama and renamed LION.
4.3.1999: Arrived at Alang for demolition by Annapurna Shipbreaking Co.

24. SISSILI RIVER 1980-1993
13,004g 7,506n
167.3 (oa) x 22.92 x 9.79 metres.
6-cyl. 2SCSA oil engines by Mitsubishi Heavy Industries Ltd., Kobe, Japan; 14,400 BHP, 18 knots.
25.10.1979: Launched by Hyundai Heavy Industries Co. Ltd., Ulsan, South Korea (Yard No. 120) for Black Star Line Ltd., Accra as SISSILI RIVER.
3.1980: Completed.
11.1993: Sold to Winter Star Marine Co. Ltd. (Hellenic Star Shipping Co. S.A.), Athens, Greece and renamed WORLD STAR under the Cyprus flag.
9.1995: Renamed LIBRA CHILE.
11.1996: Reverted to WORLD STAR.
3.2005: Sold to Four Seasons Maritime S.A. (Sinokor Merchant Marine Co. Ltd.), Seoul, South Korea and renamed GLOBAL CARRIER.
7.2005: Transferred to Sinokor Merchant Marine Co. Ltd., Seoul.
5.2007: Still in service; the last surviving Black Star ship.

Top: Volta River. [FotoFlite]
Middle: Keta Lagoon. [FotoFlite]
Bottom: Sissili River. [FotofFlite]

VESSELS BROKEN UP BY ARNOTT, YOUNG AT DALMUIR
Part 1: 1934-1962
Ian Buxton

Arnott, Young used a number prefixed 'D' for Dalmuir ships pre-war and 'T' for Troon ones, but dropped the numbers post-war. Tonnages given for merchant ships are gross, for warships deadweight (shown as 'd').
All are iron or steel steamers unless otherwise stated.
The last known operator/manager or navy is listed.
From the Second World War to 1962, all ships to be broken up were bought by the British Iron and Steel Corporation (BISCO), which allocated ships to various breakers.

D.101 CITY OF CHESTER
Passenger/cargo 5,413/1910
Ellerman Lines Ltd., London
Purchase price £5,800
Arrived 30.1.1934.

D.102 NILOS
ex *Cheniston* 1933
Cargo 4,819/1912
L.A. Embiricos, Andros
Purchase price £5,450
Arrived 9.4.1934 from Avonmouth.

D.103 MAGNETICLIGHT
ex *Magnetic* 1898
Steam lighter 39/1877
A. Millar, Greenock
Arrived 4.1934.

D.104 CITY OF CARLISLE
ex *Kathlamba* 1926
Passasenger/cargo 6,382/1913
Ellerman and Bucknall Steamship Co. Ltd., London
Purchase price £8,000
Arrived 9.6.1934 having been laid up in the Gareloch.

D.105 THE BARONESS
Dredger 238/1904
Great Western Railway Co., London
Purchase price £660
Arrived 7.1934.

D.106 EMPRESS OF FRANCE
ex *Alsatian* 1919
Passenger 18,452/1913
Canadian Pacific Steamships Ltd., Liverpool
Purchase price £33,900
Arrived 24.11.1934
Laid up in the Clyde since 9.1931 and purchased 20.10.1934
Built by Beardmore and broken up where she was fitted out.

D.107 WARRIOR
Tug 146/1903
Steel and Bennie Ltd., Glasgow
Purchase price £330
Arrived 7.1935.

The first of many, *City of Chester* in the Mersey off Birkenhead. *[J. and M. Clarkson]*
Mozart, one of the few sailing ships scrapped at Dalmuir, seen in the yard on 22nd September 1935 (below). *[J. and M. Clarkson collection]*

D.108 CAIRNDHU
Dredger 698/1892
Trustees of the Clyde Navigation, Glasgow
Purchase price £1,767
Arrived 4.1935

D.109 Four barges
Arrived 6.1935 from Whitehaven.

D.110 DREDGOL
Oiler 4,000/1918
Royal Navy
Purchase price £5,514
Arrived 8.1935 having left Rosyth 3.8.1935.

D.111 MOZART
Barkentine 1,987/1904

H. Lundqvist, Mariehamn
Purchase price £1,300
Arrived 9.1935 from Belfast.

D.112 GILBERTSON
Dredger 427/1886
Workington Harbour and Dock Board.
Purchase price £1,450
Arrived 10.1935.

D.113 JAMAICA SETTLER
ex *Highland Laddie* 1929
Refrigerated cargo 7,256/1910
Jamaica Banana Producers Steamship Co. Ltd., London
Purchase price £12,000
Arrived 26.10.1935 from London.

D.114 MATJE
ex *Prince Ja Ja* 1902
Coaster 278/1890
Monroe Brothers Ltd., Liverpool
Purchase price £400
Arrived 29.10.1935.

D.115 MOLLY
Barge
Purchase price £15
Arrived 12.1935.

D.116 PORTADOWN
Coaster 273/1900
Samuel Gray, Belfast
Purchase price £505
Arrived 12.1935 having been bought at Belfast.

D.117 SAN UGON
Tanker 5,998/1921
Compañia Mexicana de Vapores 'San Antonio' S.A., Tampico
Purchase price £8,250
Arrived 24.12.1935.

D.118 IONA
Passenger ferry 396/1864
David Macbrayne Ltd., Glasgow
Purchase price £1,262
Arrived 27.2.1936.

D.119 COLUMBA
Passenger ferry 602/1878
David Macbrayne Ltd., Glasgow
Purchase price £1,667
Arrived 27.2.1936.

D.120 LUCULLITE
Steam lighter 81/1899
James Warnock, Paisley
Purchase price £55
Arrived 4.1936.

D.121 MINNEKAHDA
Passenger/cargo 17,281/1918
Atlantic Transport Co. of West Virginia, New York
Purchase price £35,770
Arrived 29.4.1936 from New York.

Jamaica Settler. [J. and M. Clarkson collection]

Iona of 1864. [W. Robertson and Co./J. and M. Clarkson collection]

Baradine in the yard in July 1936. [John McRoberts/J. and M. Clarkson]

D.122 CONSTANCE
Cruiser 3,920/1916
Royal Navy
Purchase price £16,250
Arrived 7.1936 having left Portsmouth 25.6.1936.

D.123 BARADINE
Passenger/cargo 13,072/1921
P&O Steam Navigation Co., London
Purchase price £26,150
Arrived 4.7.1936 from London under her own steam.

D.124A ALNE No.1
Hopper barge 116/1902
Maryport Harbour Commission
Arrived 8.1936.

D.124B ALNE No.2
Hopper barge 109/1906
Maryport Harbour Commission
Arrived 8.1936.

D.124C DREDGER No.3
Dredger 153n/1906
Maryport Harbour Commission
Arrived 8.1936.

D.124D **NETHERHALL**
Tug 69/1897
Maryport Harbour Commission
Arrived 8.1936
D.124A, 124B, 124C and 124D were bought for a total of £960.

D.125A **DIANA**
Trawler 172/1899
Hewett Fishing Co. Ltd., London
Purchase price £295
Arrived 10.1936.

D.125B **PENGUIN**
Trawler 190/1902
Hewett Fishing Co. Ltd., London
Purchase price £300
Arrived 10.1936.

D.126 **LAIRDSLOCH**
ex *Partridge* 1929
Passenger/cargo 1,461/1906
Burns and Laird Lines Ltd., Glasgow
Purchase price £4,040
Arrived 10.1936.

D.127 **VASCO DA GAMA**
Coast defence 2,972d/1878
Portugese Navy
Purchase price £3,570
Arrived 12.12.1936 having been towed from Lisbon 26.11.1936 by tug *Superman*. Her engines had been removed.

D.128 **TRIAINA**
ex *Meropi* 1928, ex *Polgowan* 1922, ex *Macedonia* 1915
Cargo 4,358/1900

G.C. Lemos and M.A. Georgilis, Chios
Purchase price £7,500
Arrived 1.2.1937
Stranded Kames Bay 21.1.1937; refloated and broken up at Dalmuir.

D.129 **FLEETWOOD**
Dredger 479/1906
London, Midland and Scottish Railway Co., London
Purchase price £1,425
Arrived 2.1937.

D.130 **VIGILANT**
ex *Violet* 1894, ex *Violette* 1893, ex *Violet* 1888
Fishery cruiser 134/1886

Purchase price £650
Arrived 2.1937.

D.131 **WEXFORDIAN**
ex *Blarney* 1933, ex *Pembroke Coast* 1930, ex *Sir Roger Bacon* 1913
Coaster 809/1912
Wexford Steamship Co. Ltd., Wexford
Purchase price £1,300
Arrived 3.1937
Stranded Wexford 29.2.1936, refloated and sold for scrap.

D.132 **KIRKHAM**
Hopper barge 319/1896
London, Midland and Scottish Railway Co., London
Purchase price £825
Arrived 4.1937.

Triaina laid up at Port Bannatyne in July 1936. *[John McRoberts/J. and M. Clarkson]*

Wexfordian sailing from Birkenhead. *[John McRoberts/J. and M. Clarkson]*

Bhamo. [J. and M. Clarkson.]

D.133 MIKULA
ex *Mikula Seleaninovitch* 1923, ex *J D Hazen* 1916
Icebreaker 3,575/1916
Maritime Navigation Co. Ltd., Liverpool, Nova Scotia.
Purchase price £16,562
Arrived 16.5.1937.

D.134 CAIRNGORM
Coaster 401/1904
William Robertson, Glasgow
Purchase price £1,295
Arrived 6.1937.

D.135 SLIEVE GALLION
Cargo 1,166/1908
London, Midland and Scottish Railway Co., London
Purchase price £5,150
Arrived 6.1937.

D.136 WATCHFUL
Drifter 88/1903
James Alexander, Glasgow
Purchase price £245
Arrived 7.1937.

D.137 JOHN COULSON
ex *Archdale*, ex *Vixen*
Tug 119/1896
James Strong, Belfast
Purchase price £385
Arrived 11.1937.

D.138 SHAMROCK
Wooden lightship 96 feet, 1867
Purchase price £575
Commissioners of Irish Lights, Dublin
Sold via Samuel Gray, Belfast.

D.139 NAILSEA TOWER
ex *Chinkoa* 1937, ex *Arabistan* 1914
Cargo 5,222/1913
Nailsea Steamship Co. Ltd., Cardiff
Purchase price £12,000
Arrived 28.11.1937
This ship and the *Nailsea Vale* were acquired by Cardiff owners and broken up under the British government's 'Scrap and Build' scheme to qualify them for a loan to build the steamer *Nailsea Moor* (4,962/1937).

D.140 NAILSEA VALE
ex *Clan Macbeth* 1937
Cargo 4,647/1913
Nailsea Steamship Co. Ltd., Cardiff
Purchase price £10,750
Arrived 2.1.1938.

D.141 WEST HASSAYAMPA
Cargo 5,759/1919
United States Maritime Commission, Washington
Purchase price £18,012
Arrived 27.1.1938
Purchased 27.10.1937 and sailed from Galveston with a scrap cargo 1.1.1938.

D.142 CITY OF FORT WORTH
Cargo 6,501/1920
United States Maritime Commission, Washington
Purchase price £17,106
Arrived 23.3.1938
Purchased 1.12.1937 and sailed from Norfolk with scrap 14.2.1938.

D.143 ARDEN
Cargo 5,976/1921
United States Maritime Commission, Washington
Purchase price £15,388
Arrived 13.7.1938
Sailed from Galveston with scrap 4.4.1938 and arrived Greenock 26.4.1938.

D.144 BHAMO
Passenger/cargo 5,366/1908
W.H. Arnott, Young and Co. Ltd. who used her to carry scrap cargoes for Colvilles Ltd. Previous owner P. Henderson and Co., Glasgow
Purchase price £12,500
Arrived in the Clyde: 11.10.1938

D.145 L.69
Submarine 960d/1923
Royal Navy
Purchase price £3,510
Arrived 1.1939
Sold by 23.12.1938 and left Portsmouth 24.1.1939

D.146 HAREBELL
Sloop 1,345d/1918
Royal Navy
Purchase price £2,700
Arrived 7.2.1939.
Sold 23.12.1938 and left Devonport 3.2.1939.

D.147 L.21
Submarine 890d 1920
Royal Navy
Purchase price £3,440
Arrived 5.3.1939
Sold 23.12.1938
L.21 stranded on Arran 21.2.1939 whilst in tow from Portsmouth.

CONNEMARA
ex *Fantome* 1937, ex *Gudruda* 1902, ex *Goddess* 1898
Wooden motor yacht 180/1893 (rebuilt 1911)
Marquess of Dufferin and Ava, Clandeboye
Purchase price £1,200
Arrived 5.1939.

GLEN ROSA
Passenger ferry 306/1893
London, Midland and Scottish Railway Co., London
Purchase price £1,005
Arrived 8.1939.

GIPSY QUEEN
Excursion steamer 75/1905
James Aitken and Co. Ltd., Glasgow
Purchase price £175
Arrived 3.6.1940 from Forth and Clyde Canal.

EMPIRE GOVERNOR
ex *Esquilino* 1940
Cargo 8,657/1925
Ministry of War Transport, London
Arrived 12.1.1946
Hulk to Troon 18.4.1946.

BELLEISLE
Destroyer 2,380d/1946
Royal Navy
Arrived 18.2.1946
Incomplete hull launched by Fairfield 7.2.1946. Berthed at Dalmuir, then to Troon 2.4.1946.

CITY OF LONDON
Accomodation ship, former cargo 8,956/1907
Ellerman Lines Ltd., London
Purchase price £7,000
Arrived 5.1946
Hulk to Troon 27.9.1946.

DIOMEDE
Cruiser 4,850d/1922
Royal Navy
Arrived 13.5.1946
Left Falmouth for Dalmuir 5.5.1946 and had stranded near Penzance 8.5.1946
Hulk to Troon 4.12.1946.

SANDHURST
ex *Manipur* 1915
Royal Navy
Depot ship 11,500d/1906
Arrived 7.1946
Hulk to Troon 27.12.1946.

SULTAN
ex *Fisgard IV* 1932, ex *Sultan* 1906
Royal Navy
Training vessel, former battleship 9,290d/1871
Arrived 8.10.1946 having left Portsmouth 3.10.1946
Hulk to Troon 7.5.1947.

HMS *Harebell*, an *Anchusa* class sloop. Her greatest claim to fame was on 29th August 1930 when she took part in the evacuation of the island of St. Kilda, taking the last 33 inhabitants to the mainland. *[Rick Cox collection]*

Glen Rosa leaving Keppel Pier in July 1936. *[J. McRobers/J. and M. Clarkson]*

The troopship *City of London* laid up on the Clyde after being decommissioned. *[The Ballast Trust]*

IROQUOIS
Tanker 8,937/1907
Anglo-American Oil Co. Ltd., London
Purchase price £15,000
Arrived 1.1947
She had arrived Glasgow 4.6.1946 from Abadan
Breaking up began 6.1.1947, hulk to Troon 23.1.1947.

EMPIRE WAVENEY
ex *Milwaukee* 1945
Troopship 16,754/1929
Ministry of War Transport, London
Arrived 27.1.1947 having left Liverpool in tow 26.1.1947.
Burned out Liverpool 2.3.1946 and declared a constructive total loss
Hulk to Troon 25.9.1947.

THEMISTOCLES
Passenger/cargo 11,231/1911
Shaw, Savill and Albion Co. Ltd., London
Purchase price £29,000
Arrived 24.8.1947 having been laid up River Blackwater
Hulk to Troon 25.11.1947.

HAWKINS
Cruiser 9,800d/1919
Royal Navy
Arrived 1947/48
Arrived Troon 28.2.1948, reported as a hulk from Dalmuir but coming from Rothesay and given her 18-foot draft and use in ship target trials, it seems more likely that she went straight to Troon.

FURIOUS
Aircraft carrier 22,450d/1917
Royal Navy
Arrived 14.3.1948
Hulk to Troon 13.6.1949.

QUEEN ELIZABETH
Battleship 32,700d/1915
Royal Navy
Arrived 7.7.1948 having left Southampton Water 21.6.1948 in tow of *Englishman*, *Tradesman* and *Masterman*. Arrived Tail of the Bank 28.6.1948
Hulk to Troon 14.4.1949.

BOSWORTH
ex *War Peridot* 1920
Blockship 6,672/1919
Ministry of War Transport, London
Arrived 4.5.1949
Part of the Mulberry Harbour breakwater, refloated and towed from Arromanches 28.4.1949
Hulk to Troon 9.6.1949.

CHORAN MARU
ex *Ruthenia* 1942, ex *Regina* 1916, ex *Ruthenia* 1914, ex *Lake Champlain* 1913
Oil hulk 7,392/1900
Japanese Government
Arrived 18.6.1949
Towed from Singapore 3.4.1949 by *Englishman* for £21,000
Hulk to Troon 13.7.1949.

The depot ship HMS *Sandhurst* was completed in 1906 by Harland and Wolf at Belfast as T. and J. Brocklebank's *Manipur*. In World War One she served first as a dummy battleship HMS *Indomitable* and then as a fleet repair ship. During World War Two she was at Dover, Londonderry and finally Greenock. *[J. and M. Clarkson collection]*

Themistocles coming alongside at Liverpool on 21st May 1934. *[J. McRoberts/J. and M. Clarkson]*

HMS *Furious* was designed as a battlecruiser but converted to an aircraft carrier in 1917 and further modified in 1922/25. At this stage there was no island but one was constructed during a refit in 1939. She survived the war without any major damage but was withdrawn in 1944 due to her deteriorating condition.*[Rick Cox collection]*

NEW YORK
Passenger 21,455/1927
Hamburg-Amerika Linie, Hamburg
Purchase price £65,318
Arrived 2.8.1949
Bombed wreck raised at Kiel 1949
Towed from Kiel 19.7.1949 by *Merchantman* and *Tradesman*
Hulk to Troon 18.1.1950.

SUSSEX
Cruiser 9,830d/1929
Royal Navy
Arrived 23.2.1950 from Portsmouth
Hulk to Troon 13.6.1950.

STOIC
Submarine 715d/1943
Royal Navy
Arrived 1950?
No record of this vessel being broken up at Dalmuir. Probably scrapped by Arnott, Young at Loch Alsh where she was used in ship target trials.

CITY OF EXETER
Passenger/cargo 9,793/1914
Ellerman Lines Ltd., London
Purchase price £22,500

Top: *Bosworth* was originally owned by the Canadian Pacific Railway Company. In 1928 she was bought by H. M. Thomson of London and taken over by the Ministry of War Transport in 1944. *[J. and M. Clarkson collection]*
Middle: The engines midships tanker *Alan Clore* in the Mersey in September 1947.
Bottom: *City of Exeter* at Dalmuir 18th July 1950. *[Middle and bottom: J. McRoberts/J. and M. Clarkson.]*

Arrived 14.7.1950 having sailed from Liverpool 12.7.1950.

COLONIAL
ex *Assyria* 1929, *Ypiranga* 1920
Passenger/cargo 8,371/1908
Companhia Colonial de Navegação, Lisbon
Towed from Lisbon 7.9.1950 as BISCO 9. Broke tow and went ashore on Davaar Island, Clyde 17.9.1950
Broken up *in situ* by Arnott Young 10.1950.

ALAN CLORE
ex *Cherryleaf* 1947
Tanker 5,831/1917
Stevinson, Hardy and Co. Ltd., London
Arrived 20.12.1950 having left Falmouth 12.12.1950
Hulk to Troon 30.1.1951.

ORDUÑA
Troopship 15,507/1914
Pacific Steam Navigation Co., Liverpool
Purchase price £115,000
Arrived 31.1.1951
Hulk to Troon 17.6.1951.

ACCORDANCE
Coaster 259/1923
Aiden Shipping Co. Ltd., Glasgow
Arrived 2.1951
Breaking up began at Old Kilpatrick 15.2.1951.

CITY OF TOKIO
Cargo 6,993/1921
Ellerman Lines Ltd., London
Purchase price £52,500
Arrived 1.6.1951 having left Liverpool
31.5.1951.

TOPMAST No.4
ex *D.C.G* 1939, ex *Camber* 1922
Tug 96/1907
W.H. Arnott, Young and Co. Ltd., Glasgow
Arrived 7.1951.

KHANDALLA
Cargo 7,018/1923
British India Steam Navigation Co. Ltd.,
London
Purchase price £75,000
Arrived 24.12.1951 in tow from London
17.12.1951
Hulk to Troon 14.3.1952.

POLAR CHIEF
ex *Empire Chief* 1946, ex *Polar Chief* 1941,
ex *Anglo-Norse* 1929, ex *Rey Alfonso* 1927,
ex *Crenella* 1923, ex *Montcalm* 1916
Tanker 8,091/1897
Christian Salvesen and Co., Leith
Purchase price £120,000
Arrived 29.4.1952
Hulk to Troon 23.6.1952.

MENELAUS
Cargo 10,402/1923
Purchase price £135,000
Alfred Holt and Co., Liverpool
Arrived 25.6.1952
Hulk to Troon 29.8.1952.

DIOMED
Cargo 10,485/1922
Alfred Holt and Co., Liverpool
Purchase price £110,000
Arrived 9.1952 having been bought at
London 2.9.1952.

Above: *Orduna*. [J. and M. Clarkson]
Below: *Menelaus* in the Mersey on 19th June 1947. [J. McRoberts/J. and M. Clarkson]

ORMONDE
Pass/cargo 15,047/1917
Purchase price £195,000
Orient Steam Navigation Co. Ltd., London
Arrived 5.12.1952 having left left London
1.12.1952
Hulk to Troon 25.5.1953.

CHITRAL
Passenger/cargo 15,555/1925
P&O Steam Navigation Co., London
Purchase price £167,500
Arrived 2.4.1953 from London.

MAHANA
Refrigerated cargo 8,752/1917
Purchase price £96,500
Shaw Savill and Albion Co. Ltd., London
Arrived 31.5.1953
Hulk to Troon 15.7.1953.

AORANGI
Motor passenger/cargo 17,486/1924
Canadian Australasian Line Ltd., Vancouver
Arrived 25.7.1953
Hulk to Troon 6.4.1954.

DORELIAN
Cargo 6,640/1923
Donaldson Line Ltd., Glasgow
Purchase price £44,000
Arrived 2.1954 having arrived Glasgow
from Liverpool 18.1.1954.

Mahana. [B. and A. Feilden/J. and M. Clarkson]

DYMAS
ex *Glenbeg* 1949
Refrigerated cargo motor ship 9,461/1922
Alfred Holt and Co., Liverpool
Purchase price £54,000
Arrived 8.4.1954.
Hulk to Old Kilpatrick 3.8.1954.

SIREHAV
ex *Nordanbris* 1946, ex *Pollux* 1943
Motor tanker 8,606/1928
A.I. Langfeldt & Co., Kristiansand
Purchase price £55,000
Arrived 1.7.1954 having discharged her last cargo at Finnart in June 1954.

ANTARCTIC TANKER
ex *Brasil* 1951
Motor tanker 8,159/1935
Anton von der Lippe, London
Arrived 20.7.1954 via Faslane.

MAGNOLIA
Tanker 9,512/1935
Socony-Vacuum Oil Co. Ltd., New York
Purchase price £62,000
Arrived 11.10.1954.

SHROPSHIRE
Cruiser 9,830d/1929
Royal Navy
Purchase price £84,563
Arrived 20.1.1955
Bought by BISCO in Australia 9.1954
Towed from Sydney 9.10.1954
Hulk to Troon 19.9.1955.

BULAWAYO
ex *Northmark* 1947, ex *Nordmark* 1946, ex *Westerwald* 1939
Oiler 10,847/1939
Royal Navy
Arrived 4.10.1955 from reserve fleet in the Gareloch
Hulk to Troon 26.1.1956.

EMPIRE HALLADALE
ex *Antonio Delfino* 1932, ex *Sierra Nevada* 1934, ex *Antonio Delfino* 1946
Troopship 14,056/1922
Ministry of Transport, London
Arrived 1.2.1956.

ALACRITY
Frigate 1,430d/1945
Royal Navy
Arrived 15.9.1956 in tow from Lisahally
Hulk to Troon 3.11.1956.

INDEFATIGABLE
Aircraft carrier 26,000d/1944
Royal Navy
Arrived 4.11.1956 having been laid up Gareloch since 1954
Hulk to Troon 2.9.1957.

EMPIRE KEN
ex *Ubena* 1945
Troopship 9,523/1928
Ministry of Transport, London
Arrived 20.9.1957 from Southampton
Hulk to Troon 16.12.1957.

HMS *Shropshire* was built and scrapped at Dalmuir. Following the loss of the HMAS *Canberra* in August 1942, *Shropshire* was loaned to the Australian Navy. After seeing action in the Pacific she was present at the Japanese surrender at Tokyo Bay on 2nd September 1945. *[Rick Cox collection]*

Above: Troopship *Empire Halladale* on the Mersey, 12th May 1951. Taken as a prize at Copenhagen in May 1945 as *Sierra Nevada*, she was brought to Britain and converted for use as a troopship. *[John McRoberts/J. and M. Clarkson collection]*
Below: Sailing from Portsmouth in November 1944, HMS *Indefatigable* was another ship which saw service in the Pacific. After suffering considerable damage and casualties from Kamikaze attacks her planes took part in the last air combat of the Second World War. She returned to Europe and was placed in reserve in December 1946 at Portsmouth. *[Rick Cox collection]*

KING GEORGE V
Battleship 35,000d/1940
Royal Navy
Arrived 20.1.1958 having been laid up Gareloch since 1950
Hulk to Troon 20.5.1959.

SHIELDHILL
Dredger 787/1906
Trustees of the Clyde Navigation, Glasgow
Purchase price £5,250
Arrived 5.1959.

Arnott, Young was one of only three British shipbreakers who could handle a battleship. After lying at Tail of the Bank for 12 days, HMS *King George V* (above) is readied for her final voyage to Dalmuir on 20th January 1958, with tugs *Wrestler* (left) and *Campaigner* leading. *[Bill Green]*

The aircraft maintenance carrier HMS *Unicorn* with tugs in the Clyde. During the Second World War she served with the Home Fleet, in the Mediterranean and Pacific theatres. From June 1950 to October 1953 HMS *Unicorn* played an important part in the Korean War. *[Author's collection]*

UNICORN
Aircraft carrier 14,750d/1943
Royal Navy
Arrived 15.6.1959 having left Devonport 11.6.1959 in tow of *Welshman* and *Tradesman*
Hulk to Troon 29.3.1960.

GRAB HOPPER BARGE No.1
Hopper barge 92/---
Purchase price £340
Arrived 11.1959
To Old Kilpatrick.

PLOVER
Barge
Arrived 12.1959
To Old Kilpatrick.

SALACIA
Motor cargo 5,572/1937
Donaldson Line Ltd., Glasgow
Purchase price £64,500
Arrived 20.3.1960.

HIGHLAND MONARCH
Motor passenger/cargo 14,216/1928
Royal Mail Lines Ltd., London
Purchase price £190,000
Arrived 28.4.1960.

SUPERB
Cruiser 8,800d/1945
Royal Navy
Arrived 8.8.1960 having been laid up Gareloch since 1957
Hulk to Troon 16.5.1961.

LORD ANSON
Drifter 100/1927
William Picton, Milford Haven
Purchase price £800
Arrived 7.11.1960
To Old Kilpatrick.

JAMAICA
Cruiser 8,000d/1942
Royal Navy
Arrived 20.12.1960 having been laid up Gareloch since 1957
Hulk to Troon 30.5.1962.

CHINDIT
Puffer 74/1945
Cowal Coal and Trading Co. Ltd., Glasgow
Arrived 4.1961.

TOMOCYCLUS
ex *Capitol Reef* 1947
T2-type tanker 10,706/1944
Anglo-Saxon Petroleum Co. Ltd., London
Purchase price £70,000
Arrived 26.5.1961 in tow from Lough Swilly
To Old Kilpatrick 8.1961.

CLYDE II
ex *Clyde* 1961
Tug 187/1912
Trustees of the Clyde Navigation, Glasgow
Purchase price £1,550
Arrived 17.4.1961
Broken up at Old Kilpatrick.

VEHICULAR FERRYBOAT No.1
ex *Whiteinch* 1913, ex *Finnieston* 1900
Ferry 236/1890
Trustees of the Clyde Navigation, Glasgow
Purchase price £4,900
Arrived 29.6.1961
To Old Kilpatrick 8.1961.

HMS *Superb* at Dalmuir 11th August 1960. *[Rick Cox collection]*

Chindit in 1956. *[J. and M. Clarkson]*

Tomocyclus about to be towed from Lough Swilly by Steel and Bennie tugs, *Vanguard* leads, *Cruiser* alongside. She arrived at Dalmuir on 26th May 1961. Shell sold several more of their T2 tankers for about £70,000 each. *[Bill Green]*

SAN LEONARDO
ex *Turbinellus* 1949, ex *Bryce Canyon* 1947
T2-type tanker 10,641/1944
Eagle Oil and Shipping Co. Ltd., London
Purchase price £70,000
Arrived 2.9.1961.

THELICONUS
ex *Palo Duro* 1947
T2-type tanker 10,691/1944
Anglo-Saxon Petroleum Co. Ltd., London
Purchase price £70,000
Arrived 29.5.1962.

BRITISH DUKE
Motor tanker 8,562/1948
British Tanker Co. Ltd., London
Arrived 17.7.1962 after discharging at Milford Haven 12.7.1962.

BARCLOSE
Boom defence vessel 730d/1941
Royal Navy
Arrived 8.8.1962.

WOOLWICH
Submarine depot ship 8,750d/1935
Royal Navy
Arrived 18.10.1962 from Devonport
To Old Kilpatrick 3.1963.

ANDROS FIGHTER
ex *Centaur* 1957, ex *Harpoon* 1954, ex *Carlinian* 1950, ex *Ward Hunt* 1948
Liberty-type cargo 7,233/1943
Jackson Steamship Co., Monrovia
Arrived 4.1963
Last ship to be broken up for BISCO.

(To be concluded)

In the aftermath of the Suez Crisis tanker owners decided that their smaller tankers had to be replaced by much larger tankers. By 1960 the larger newbuildings were being delivered and disposal of the older, smaller ships began hence the increase in tankers at Dalmuir and other yards. *San Leonardo* (top), *Theliconus* (middle) and *British Duke* (bottom) were all relatively young when scrapped. *[Top and middle: Ships in Focus, bottom: J. and M. Clarkson collection]*

THE GREAT CEMENT ARMADA
Text and photos by Malcolm Cranfield

The West African country of Nigeria has had an eventful history. In the early 19th century, the Fulani leader Usman dan Fodio launched an Islamic crusade that brought most of the Hausa states under the loose control of an empire centered in Sokoto but in 1903 Britain took Sokoto and ended the Fulani Empire. On 1st October 1960 the Federation of Nigeria achieved independence from the British Empire and the constitution of the Federal Republic of Nigeria was adopted on 1st October 1963. At the same time, Nigeria became a member of the Commonwealth and Dr Nnamdi Azikiwe took office as Nigeria's first President.

On 15th January 1966, a group of officers led by General Yakubu Gowon (born 1934) overthrew the Government and then in May 1967 Lieutenant-Colonel Emeka Ojukwu, the military governor of the Eastern Region, declared the independence of the Republic of Biafra, an act which led to a civil war which lasted until 1970.

Prior to the civil war the cement factories of the Federation could keep up with the demand and new plants were steadily coming on stream. Occasional import licences were issued but these were usually for special categories of cement for construction projects. Although much of Nigeria was untouched by the civil war, economic development came to a virtual halt.

During the leadership of General Gowon, the volume of corruption surrounding 'The Army Boys' was restrained and primarily involved a trade in import licences which had, during the civil war, been used to conserve the foreign exchange reserves. Thus once Biafra had passed into history there was a pent-up demand for all categories of imported goods and commodities

Cement orders
The sudden increased value of Nigeria's oil reserves in the early 1970s fuelled the country's economic boom. Wartime import embargoes were lifted and foreign exchange controls relaxed. The demand for cement and other building materials became astronomical. Under pressure from the military the Government committed itself to a massive barrack building programme and ordered 16 million metric tonnes of Portland cement for the Ministry of Defence alone, amounting to 80% of the country's total cement imports. Building was taking place in an unrestricted manner throughout the country and included the main roads and bridges linking the various suburbs of Lagos, which were all being built or rebuilt simultaneously by the German contractor Julius Berger.

Import licences for cement became much in demand. The army, corrupt from lance corporals upwards, soon realised this and, with the issuing bureaucrats taking their cut, licences for quantities of cement became a tradable and bankable item. Merchant importers who may never have sold or even seen a bag of cement in their business lives were, by 1973, placing orders for bagged cement by the ship load. It is alleged that a major scandal took place, involving the purchase of construction materials at prices well above market values, but the impact of such corruption was compounded by inefficiencies.

The very limited port reconstruction which had taken place following the civil war was grossly inadequate to meet Nigeria's unanticipated new wealth. Cargo traffic far exceeded the capacity of the ports and the 1960s-era narrow roads and bridges were collapsing under the weight of road haulage. During the civil war Port Harcourt had been closed to foreign shipping, leaving Lagos (Apapa) as the only port available for the country's predominantly military needs. Hence the government acquired the smaller ports of Warri, Burutu and Calabar along with Koko and Bonny, but they had very limited discharging facilities.

The armada gathers
Lagos/Apapa is located on a series of islands, the most important being Lagos Island. Ikoyi and Victoria Islands have

The second of two examples of former British motor tramps built by Lithgows Ltd. which were anchored off Lagos at Christmas 1975 (see page 65).

The *Cosmaria* (right) dated from 1954 as Lyle Shipping's *Cape Grenville*. Her Glasgow owners sold her in 1965 and she initially became *Cosmar* before renaming *Cosmaria* in 1973. She had arrived from Spain on 28th June 1975, and sailed after discharge in February 1976. The ship had several years of trading left, and was to carry the names *Selas*, *Naya* and *Mayfair* before being broken up at Gadani Beach in 1980.

some of the more expensive residential housing while the Port of Apapa lies across the bay. The sprawling urban area on the mainland includes Ikeja, where the airport is situated. The port was in desperate need of modernization but the machinery and parts ordered were slow to arrive, in part because they were held up in ships unable to dock. No-one had foreseen what would happen if construction materials such as cement arrived ahead of the port improvements.

At a time when the combined handling capacity of Nigerian ports was only 6.5 million tonnes of general cargo per annum, the Government had expected 16 million metric tonnes of cement to be delivered within twelve months.

Nigerian ports capable of handling ships other than large tankers are notoriously prescriptive in their limitations of draught and dimensions: 10,000 tonnes was, with luck, the largest stem of cement that could be handled in the biggest port, Lagos/Apapa. Even for all commodities together, the discharging capacity at Lagos/Apapa was less than two million metric tonnes a year.

Rotation of which ships berthed and when was handled by the self-administrating group of ships' agents who, until 1975, were able to defy political interference. Although Brigadier Adekunle, the Military Port Commandant of Lagos, was given full emergency powers to decongest the port, this had little effect.

By 1976 the only way to get general cargo into Nigeria was by either using the ships and services of the conference lines (and paying a hefty congestion surcharge) or using the growing fleet of 1,000 deadweight 'small Danes' (and others such as Crescent's *Dangeld* of 1969) which could land cargo literally at beach-heads in lagoons and the Niger Delta's oil rivers. It is alleged that Nigerian customs officials were appropriately 'dashed' to agree to these informal ports. This was a particularly important conduit for building materials and fittings which had sufficient value to bear the freight/charter costs and were used along with some of that cement.

Although the well-known liner companies such as Elder Dempster were given some priority to bring into Nigeria essential products and served its export markets, the congestion tended to advance the pace of change towards containerised and ro-ro operations, and the Conference Lines' fleets of cargo liners were displaced and sold. Nigerian National's own *Dan Fodio* of 1950, renamed *Fos*, was one such vessel used for the carriage of cement.

By April 1975 there were about one hundred ships, growing by June to four hundred of which around three quarters were carrying a total of around 2.5 million tonnes of cement, anchored off waiting to unload at Apapa port where there were just six berths plus a similar number of mid-stream buoys for discharging cement into barges. During this period it was estimated that, on average, $4,100 per day was being paid in demurrage for each cement vessel delayed over ten days and that the average waiting time was 180 days. Many ships waited up to a year to discharge and, but for this opportunity, they may well have been either in lay up or at breakers' yards.

More pilferable cargoes than cement were also delayed. Thus, between arrival at anchor on 11th December 1975 and berthing in Lagos port on 22nd May 1976, the entire cargo of 90,000 cartons of beer on board the steamer *Melic Sun* (the former *Devonbrook* of 1954) was looted.

In all, Nigeria executed 109 cement procurement contracts valued at almost one billion dollars with 68 suppliers in a variety of countries, mainly Eastern Bloc (the Soviet Union, Poland and Romania), plus Greece, Italy and Spain. State-owned cement manufacturers in Eastern Europe were only too happy to expand production to meet this new outlet, particularly for negotiable hard currency.

The contracts required Nigeria to issue letters of

Upper: The Cypriot-flag *Fos* had been one of Nigerian National Lines' earliest ships, *Dan Fodio*, and before that Buries Markes' *La Sierra*, built 1950. In 1978 *Fos* was renamed *Kronos I*, then *Kronos II*, and in October of that year broken up at Gadani Beach.

Lower: *Melic Sun* owned by the Melic Shipping Co. of Ghana was originally Comben Longstaff's *Devonbrook*. Although built as late as 1954, and with the lines of a motor ship, she was in fact a steamer. Comben Longstaff sold her in 1963 when she became Watson's *Lady Sylvia*. She ran as *Tolmi* from 1968 until she became *Melic Sun* in 1974. Renamed *The Word* she was wrecked one nautical mile off Takoradi on 25th April 1979.

credit for the amount due under each contract. Once the cargo was loaded, insured and sailing to Nigeria, payment would be made. The contracts also provided for demurrage which would be paid if a ship was detained in Nigerian waters.

Unfortunately, by the time some of the cement ships had berthed, their cargo had spoiled as, due to the chemical composition of the cement, much of it was unusable for building after six months from manufacture. Some ships therefore did not even make it to the port but sank by accident or design once their cargoes became damp and waterlogged.

Spoiled and inferior-grade cement was often concealed by mixing it with acceptable material for use in public building projects. Later, buildings collapsed or had to be dismantled because of the inferior product. Some new roads were washed away because of bad construction and inadequate controls.

There was the story of a Norwegian owner who took delivery of a new building, geared, single-decker several months ahead of the start of a long-term affreightment contract. Seizing the chance of a quick remunerative fixture the ship was loaded down to her marks with 6,000 tonnes for Lagos. Cement is hygroscopic and the tropical Nigerian coastline is very humid for most of the year. When the owner recovered his ship two years later she was declared a constructive total loss as her cement cargo had, in the process of waiting to be discharged, gone solid in parts, straining and distorting the steel structure in the cargo areas – and this on her maiden voyage!

Solutions
Following a military coup on 30th July 1975 during which Brigadier Murtala Mohammed ousted General Gowon, immediate action was taken to halt the cement armada. On 9th August 1975 Nigeria's Ports Authority issued Government Notice No. 1434, a regulation which stated that, effective from 18th August, all ships destined for Lagos/Apapa would be required to convey to the Ports Authority, two months before sailing, certain information concerning their time of arrival in the port. Then, on 18th August, Nigeria cabled its suppliers and asked them to stop sending cement, and to cease loading, or even chartering, ships.

But as this measure was acting too slowly to reduce the number of ships on demurrage, Nigeria took another crucial step in September 1975. In a desperate effort to find relief, Nigeria revoked the supposedly irrevocable letters of credit from the Nigerian Central Bank that backed the purchases in the first place. This move caused problems for international traders and may have bankrupted some producers, shippers and shipowners. The most celebrated legal case, although one in which no evidence of corruption was adduced, was that of Trendtex Corporation versus Central Bank in which the rights of shipowners to demurrage were tested in court.

Then, almost three months later, on 19th December 1975, Nigeria promulgated Decree No. 40, a law prohibiting entry into a Nigerian port to any ship which had not secured two months' prior approval, and imposing criminal penalties for unauthorized entry.

Murtala Muhammad's rule was short-lived: he was assassinated during an unsuccessful coup d'état by Lieutenant-Colonel B.S. Dimka in February 1976 and the country went into deep mourning and decline. By that time the queue of ships outside Lagos had stabilized but the effects of his decisive action to address the causes of the congestion necessarily took several months to take effect.

On 11th September 1976 'Lloyds List' reported that '…after the chaotic conditions which existed for so long in Nigeria, charterers are back in the market for tonnage for cement'. With the construction of new barge piers in Kiri Kiri creek allowing up to 7,000 tonnes per day to be discharged, the queue had been reduced to 60 ships.

Photographing the ships
The writer was aware that the familiar tramp ships, particularly those built during or soon after the Second World War in British and other European shipyards, were fast disappearing. Working at the time for Barber Lines in Oslo, I took advantage of the Jahre Line ferry connection to Kiel where these and other interesting ships could be seen transiting the Kiel Canal.

However, more and more vessels, including those loading cement in Poland for Nigeria, were sailing around the Skaw instead of transiting the Kiel Canal. If I were to fly to Nigeria I could photograph the ships at anchor off Lagos, and not just those which had arrived from Poland but also from the Black Sea, and those with other cargoes from elsewhere in Europe and further afield.

The timing seemed right after Christmas 1975, when the queue of ships was at its height and the weather conditions were at their seasonal best, to undertake the risky visit to Lagos.

It was only with the help of Palm Line Agencies, agents for Barber Lines in Nigeria, that I was able to hire a boat for eight hours on 4th January 1976 and so photograph over one hundred of the oldest vessels still afloat in the 20 square-mile designated anchorage. The scene in Lagos Roads was akin to pictures of Second World War convoys. Vessels discharging at the buoys in Lagos harbour were also successfully photographed during brief boat hires on New Year's Eve and New Year's Day.

The main target vessel, *Sas* (ex Common Brothers' *Hindustan* of 1940), was anchored off closest of all to the breakwater, having returned on 5th November 1975 after an earlier call during the planning stage of my visit.

The day started poorly with a thick fog, which made the initial photographs of *Sas* somewhat disappointing, but the fog lifted quickly as the sun rose and in fact prevented the heat haze from becoming as strong and oppressive as usual. *Sas* remained at anchor until 5th July 1976 when she sailed to Abidjan for stores before berthing at Apapa/Lagos around 15th July and eventually sailing from the port on 29th September 1976. After a series of engine problems, and lengthy periods of lay up at Sete and at her home port of Piraeus, she was scrapped at Santander in July 1979.

Once the mist lifted, the full extent of the anchorage became apparent with the targeted former British or British-built ships surrounding us as far as the eye could see. A course was plotted between them, with my signalling to the boat skipper to head not directly towards each one but to an adjacent vessel so that his course would take the boat at a suitable distance for photography.

Ships in the queue which required stores or bunkers could not obtain them locally so were obliged to sail the short distance to Abidjan, Ivory Coast, and return to the

A fine view of *Sas*, the former Common Brothers' motor ship *Hindustan* built in 1940. She had also carried the name *Almen* from 1954 to 1963. *Sas* wore the funnel colours of owner G.Th. Sigalas of Piraeus.

anchorage to await berthing instructions which, in some cases, never came. Giles Large, who suffered 18 days waiting in the anchorage in May 1976 on board the Danish ro-ro *Sussex*, had reported that radio communications with ships' agents were very difficult and that hopelessly optimistic berthing prospects were commonplace.

After covering an area west of the breakwaters it was around midday when we approached *Sas* again, by then bathed in glorious sunshine. Our boat's crew would have returned to port at that point had we not observed a further vast area of shipping anchored to the north, close to the coast, including what was clearly Gulf Shipping's *Confidence Express*, the former Houlder Brothers' *Swan River* of 1959. She had arrived on 15th September 1975 from the Black Sea and was reported to have left the anchorage the following day to take on stores at Abidjan. After a further call at Abidjan in May, she eventually discharged and sailed for Piraeus on 20th July 1976. *Confidence Express* in fact outlived most of the vessels seen at anchor on 4th January 1976, being renamed twice during the following nine years' ownership by Gulf Shipping before being scrapped in India. Anchored close by were the same owners' vessels, *Gulf Reliance* (ex *Tremeadow* of 1958) and *Al-Karim* (ex *Riverdore* of 1959). This superb group of vessels bathed in the afternoon sunshine included many more of interest, the most notable being *Peramataris* (ex *Empire Rennie* of 1941). She had sailed from the Black Sea in May 1975, passing Istanbul on the 30th, and called at Piraeus on 3rd June for stores,

Upper: *Confidence Express*, ex *Premier Atlantic* in 1973, was the former Houlder Brothers' *Swan River* of 1959. She survived her cement voyage to become *Bachlong* in 1979 and *Eastern Concord* in 1980 as which she arrived at Bombay for scrapping in January 1983.

Lower: *Gulf Reliance*, ex *Reliance Express* in 1975, started life as Hain's *Tremeadow* in 1958. The tiny letters of her name contrast with the large letter G for Gulf Shipping on her funnel. She was broken up at Kaohsiung in May 1980.

One of the author's most prized photographs from his Lagos visit was that of *Peramataris*. Built in 1941 as *Empire Rennie*, from 1942 she had Dutch owners as *Frans Hals* and *Alchiba* until 1956 when Hansa Line bought her and renamed her *Rheinfels*. She became *Peramataris* in 1968. The additional king posts mark her out as a far from standard Empire ship.

bunkers or a crew change. On 6th June she was reported to have caught fire and was abandoned by her crew east of Malta but was later reboarded and put in to Augusta, Sicily. Contrary to the report in the second edition of Mitchell and Sawyers' 'The Empire Ships', *Peramataris* was not laid up at Augusta but sailed soon afterwards, passing Gibraltar on 20th June 1975. She had been anchored off Apapa/Lagos since 17th July 1975 and must have discharged her cargo during May or June 1976 as she arrived back at Piraeus on 11th July 1976, where she was finally laid up. She did not sail again and was scrapped locally in February 1979.

Meanwhile, the 1956 Bartram-built *Astyanax*, which had arrived from Gdynia on 5th November, had still not discharged her cargo a year later when she suffered a mysterious engine room fire at Abidjan on Christmas Eve 1976 and was eventually scuttled off that port on 18th November 1977.

Other ships were also lost in mysterious circumstances, some with cargo intact, including the Cyprus-flagged *Pati* of 1950, also photographed at anchor on 4th January 1976. Her owners were A. Halcoussis and Co., operators of an interesting fleet including several ships which had been insurance write-offs. Formerly *Kate A* and before that *Ajana* of Australind, *Pati* was shown at Lagos in the very first issue of 'Record'.

The cement cargo on board *Pati* had been loaded at Novorossisk in the Black Sea in October 1975 and appears to have been resold to a consignee in Dubai when she grounded on 29th February 1976 in Algoa Bay on the western edge of Thunderbolt Reef, half a mile off Cape Recife lighthouse near Port Elizabeth. Her wreck was described as 'a beautiful dive since the cargo of cement forms a colorful artificial reef, normally teeming with fish as well as lots of interesting artifacts'.

Astyanax, formerly *Maria K* until 1967 and before that *Maria C*, was one of several ships that were never to get away from west Africa: she was scuttled off Abidjan in 1977. The Greek letter L on her funnel denotes owners Costas G. and George K. Lemos.

Arosa, formerly Livanos' *Atlantic General* of 1956. Like several other ships in the anchorage, at least one of her boats is missing having been used to take the crew ashore.

Another Cyprus-flag casualty was the *Arosa* (ex *Atlantic General* of 1956), owned by Pateras Brothers. She had arrived off Apapa/Lagos in October 1975 and subsequently sailed about 8th June 1976 but grounded approximately 32 kilometres north of Hondeklip Bay, reportedly bound for Cape Town for dry docking.

Kavo Peiratis (ex Pacific Steam's *Potosi* of 1955) may have been the only one of the vessels photographed to have sailed direct to breakers following discharge. She had arrived, probably as a bunkering stop, from Benghazi in September 1975, eventually sailing on 16th August 1976 to Warri for discharge and then on to the Clyde for breaking up, arriving at Dalmuir on 13th October 1976.

Costantis II (ex Moss Hutchison's *Kantara* of 1947), spelt as *Constantis II* in all official records, had anchored off on 21st June 1975 on arrival from the Black Sea and eventually sailed to Port Harcourt on 18th March 1976 to discharge her cargo.

Antonis, which had been launched at Amsterdam on 15th July 1944 as the German *Gutenfels* but scuttled in the North Sea Canal, salvaged by Holland and renamed *Heelsum*, had arrived off Lagos from Italy on 16th June 1975. She sailed later on New Year's Day 1976, the day I photographed her on discharge buoys in Lagos harbour. She subsequently arrived at Gadani Beach on 14th February 1979 for breaking up.

Minoutsi, similarly war-built in Holland and launched as *Frankenfels* on 22nd November 1944, was left

Top: *Kavo Peiratis* of Gourdomichalis, readily recognizable as Pacific Steam's turbine steamer *Potosi* of 1952. She still looks reasonably smart, although from Lagos she went straight to the breakers.

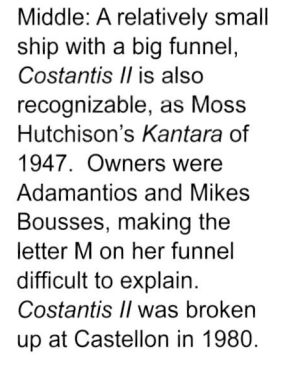

Middle: A relatively small ship with a big funnel, *Costantis II* is also recognizable, as Moss Hutchison's *Kantara* of 1947. Owners were Adamantios and Mikes Bousses, making the letter M on her funnel difficult to explain. *Costantis II* was broken up at Castellon in 1980.

Bottom: *Antonis* just before she sailed on 1st January 1976. The letter V on her funnel denotes owners Valmas Shipping Ltd.

Minoutsi was actually discharging her cargo when photographed. The distinctive design of her intended owners, DDG Hansa, is apparent. She was completed as *Albireo* and from 1963 to 1966 carried the name *Procyon*.

in a heavily damaged state on the German evacuation of Holland in 1945 and completed in 1948 as *Albireo*. She was turned round at Lagos in a mere four months, having arrived from Greece on 3rd October 1975, and sailed for Barcelona on 6th January 1976. In 1978 she was renamed *Lasia* for a single voyage to breakers in Kaohsiung where she arrived on 16th April 1980.

Nordwind, built at Flensburg in 1958, was no stranger to long periods of idleness, having been trapped in the Great Bitter Lake on the Suez Canal between 1967 and 1974. She had arrived off Lagos from Bilbao on 17th August 1975, called at Lome in nearby Togo for stores in February 1976 and is believed to have discharged at Warri in July 1976.

Irenes Banner (ex *Loradore* '58 of Michalinos), owned by Tsakos Shipping and Trading but seemingly

Uniquely amongst ships illustrated here, Great Bitter Lakes survivor *Nordwind* of 1958 had not carried a previous name. In 1979 owners 'Nordstern' Reederei sold her and she became *Rodanthi A* and a few months later *Centaurus*. She was broken up at Shanghai in 1985.

Irenes Banner was built at West Hartlepool in 1958 as *Loradore*, part of the UK fleet of Michalinos and Co. Ltd. Other previous names were *Aliartos* from 1960 to 1966 and *Thomas A* from 1970 to 1975.

on charter to a company named Irish Marine, had arrived from Greece on 11th July 1975. It is unclear where she discharged her cargo as a reported arrival at Lagos on 11th February 1976 was followed by a call at Warri in March. Two years later she caught fire while discharging another cement cargo, this time at Dawes Island, Port Harcourt, and was beached there on 22nd January 1978.

Vessels operated by the same owner would often be anchored together. This feature concludes with a typical group, *Kanaris*, *Elli 2* and *Toulla*, three former King Line vessels. It is assumed that the purpose of this practice was to minimize crew watch-keeping costs. As these and other photographs' show, ships' lifeboats were often missing as they had been used to ferry crews between ship and shore.

Three former King Line motor ships together at Lagos were *Kanaris*, ex *King Malcolm* 1972 (top); *Elli 2*, ex *King Alexandra* 1972 (middle); and *Toulla*, ex *King Arthur* 1972 (bottom). The first two were built in 1952, and *King Arthur* in 1953, all by Harland and Wolff. The letters VH denote owner Vassos Hajioannou, who traded as Alassia Steamship Co. Ltd..

PALM LINE'S TANKERS

The features on Palm Line in 'Record' 35 and 36 set out specifically to cover the company's dry cargo vessels. As reader L. Parry of Bristol has reminded us, this was not the complete story, as Palm also ran a number of vegetable oil tankers, on one of which he worked.

The decision to operate tankers in the West African trade was taken by Palm's predecessor United Africa Co. Ltd. In 1936 they took delivery of the diesel-engined *Congonian* (4,928/1936) from Howaldstwerke A.G., Hamburg and the steam-driven *Matadian* (4,275/1936) from Swan, Hunter and Wigham Richardson Ltd. at Wallsend. Both were sunk by German submarines off West Africa. *Congonian* was torpedoed by *U 65* whilst bound in ballast from Liverpool to Freetown on 18th November 1940 and sank with the loss of one life. *Matadian* was torpedoed by *U 66* on 20th March 1944 bound for the UK from Port Harcourt and Lagos with palm oil.

A replacement *Congonian* (6,082/1942) was built by Swan, Hunter and Wigham Richardson Ltd. With merchant shipbuilding under close government control during wartime, owners were normally given licenses to build their own ships only if they ordered repeats of existing vessels which required little design work. At 430 feet overall, the 1942 *Congonian* was not a repeat of the 397-feet *Matadian* (1), and neither did she match the dimensions of any of the standard designs of tanker being built. It must be assumed that the importance of the trade allowed United Africa to have a purpose-built tanker designed. In 1948 a replacement for the first *Matadian* was completed to the same dimensions as the second *Congonian*, but somewhat perversely the order had been given to Sir James Laing and Sons Ltd. who produced a distinctly different design. When the United Africa fleet was transferred to Palm Line in 1949, *Congonian* (2) became *Opobo Palm* and *Matadian* (2) (6,246/1948) became *Matadi Palm* (1). Both were to remain in the fleet until the 1960s.

A third tanker joined the fleet in 1953. The *Tema Palm* (6,178/1953) was built by A.G. Weser at Bremerhaven and was initially owned by German subsidiary Ölhandel und Transport GmbH of Hamburg. She was of a similar size to the existing tankers, and like them had a triple-expansion steam engine. This obsolescent machinery was specified so that steam from the boilers could be used to heat the vegetable oil cargo to allow it to be pumped readily. In 1960 *Tema Palm* was transferred to Palm Line ownership and the British flag, an event commemorated by her being renamed *Makurdi Palm*, rather unnecessarily one would have thought.

Sale of the 19-year-old *Opobo Palm* in 1961 seems to have taken Palm Line's planners by surprise, as there was no time to order a replacement. Fortunately, with the rapid increase in tanker size, smaller post-war vessels were available, and the *British Rover* was bought and renamed *Makeni Palm* (6,137/1951). Mr Parry joined her on the Manchester Ship Canal in September 1963, and recalls how the deck crew worked hours of overtime cleaning what appeared to be congealed lard from her tank sides. The mate hoped that this would allow palm oil to be loaded on arrival in West Africa, but the shoreside superintendent was not satisfied and ordered the tanks to be steam cleaned. The last port for loading was Boma in the Congo, where the civil war meant no shore leave. From there *Makeni Palm* sailed for Hamburg and Purfleet.

The last Palm Line tanker, the second *Matadi Palm* (8,870/1970), was completed by Swan Hunter Shipbuilders Ltd. at the former Furness yard at Haverton Hill-on-Tees. Her tanks were subdivided so that she could carry 28 different parcels of vegetable oil, so that the different types and grades of palm, palm kernel and groundnut oil could be kept separate,

The first Palm Line tanker, the *Congonian* of 1936 was torpedoed in 1940. *[Newall Dunn collection]*

as well as consignments for different merchants. *Matadi Palm* (2) saw out the independent existence of Palm Line, and in an interesting reversal of earlier policy was transferred to UAC International Ltd. in 1985 and her name shortened to *Matadi*. But this lasted for barely a year, and in 1986 she was sold with almost all other Palm Line ships. As noted below her photograph on page 201 of 'Record' 36, she was renamed *Lian* and broken up in 1995.

One of the few known views of the short-lived *Matadian* (1), taken by John McRoberts on the Mersey on 20th May 1939 (above). She was completed on the Tyne in 1936 and torpedoed in 1944. Fortunately, no lives were lost when she was sunk, but the chief officer was injured when blown off the bridge. *[Real Photographs/Roy Fenton collection]*

The second *Congonian* (above right), in war-time colours. *[Newall Dunn collection]*

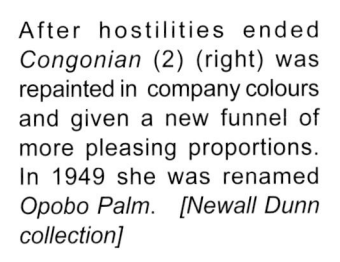

After hostilities ended *Congonian* (2) (right) was repainted in company colours and given a new funnel of more pleasing proportions. In 1949 she was renamed *Opobo Palm*. *[Newall Dunn collection]*

123

The 1942-built *Opobo Palm* (above), the former *Congonian* (2). The good outfit of derricks fore and aft indicated the presence of dry cargo holds. She ran for Palm Line until 1961 when she was sold to Hong Kong owners as *Winwar* and was broken up locally in 1963. *[Ships in Focus]*

Two views of the *Matadian* (2) (middle and below) completed in 1948 and renamed *Matadi Palm* in 1949. *[Both: Newall Dunn collection]*

The *Matadi Palm* steamed on only until February 1963 when at the tender age of 15 she left Liverpool for a breakers' yard in Spain. [*FotoFlite/J. and M. Clarkson collection*]

The German-built *Makurdi Palm* (below) ex *Tema Palm* (right) was clearly a development of the *Matadi Palm* of 1948. She was sold to Spanish owners in 1969, renamed *Santamar* and broken up in 1976. [*Right: Ships in Focus, below: FotoFlite/J. and M. Clarkson collection*]

Makeni Palm, photographed in September 1965 (below), had been built by J.L. Thompson and Sons Ltd. at Sunderland for the British Tanker Co. Ltd. Completed in 1951 as *British Rover* (right) and fitted with a Doxford oil engine she was bought by Palm Line in 1961 as something of a stop gap. *Makeni Palm* was sold in 1967 to Paris-based Greek owners who renamed her *Kerkennah*. A change of nominal owner and flag in 1972 saw her become *Palau*, as which she was broken up in 1978. *[Both: J. and M. Clarkson collection]*

SOURCES AND ACKNOWLEDGEMENTS

We thank all who gave permission for their photographs to be used, and for help in finding photographs we are particularly grateful to Tony Smith, Jim McFaul and David Whiteside of the World Ship Photo Library; to Ian Farquhar, F.W. Hawks, Peter Newall, William Schell, George Scott; and to David Hodge and Bob Todd of the National Maritime Museum, and other museums and institutions listed.

Research sources have included the *Registers* of William Schell and Tony Starke, *Lloyd's Register*, *Lloyd's Confidential Index*, *Lloyd's War Losses*, *Mercantile Navy Lists*, *Marine News* and *Shipbuilding and Shipping Record*. Use of the facilities of the World Ship Society's Central Record, the Guildhall Library, the Public Record Office and Lloyd's Register of Shipping are gratefully acknowledged, and Dr Malcolm Cooper is thanked for checking Second World War losses. Particular thanks also to Heather Fenton for editorial and indexing work, and to Marion Clarkson for accountancy services.

THE GREAT CEMENT ARMADA
Thanks to Andrew Bell. Sources include Peter Jones 'Nigeria - Boom Times' (1975-1979); Giles Large: 'Marooned Misery' in *Freighting World* 19.5.76; *Time Magazine* 'The Cement Block'; Texas Trading and Milling Corp. vs. Federal Republic of Nigeria.

FROM THE BOSUN'S LOCKER
John Clarkson

Here we have a further selection of puzzles for you to identify. Some are from our own files along with two from a reader in Germany. We hope you enjoy the challenge. First of all we have the feedback from the pictures in 'Record' 37. We had results on three of the pictures but surprisingly nothing at all on the riverside view.

Photo 1/37
David Asprey identifies this vessel as the Tynemouth to South Shields ferry *Aileen*, owned by the Tyne Ferry Company, and built by Armstrong, Whitworth as yard number 671 in 1897. She had a sister named *Audrey* (yard number 670) which later went to work as a ferry in Cork, served the Admiralty during the First World War and was later sold to the New Medway Steam Packet Co. Ltd.

Photo 2/37
Ian Farquhar tells us that the *Beagle* on page 64 was employed as a lighter at Cossack, in northern Western Australia. The photo shows her after the great cyclone had swept through on 2nd April 1898. This storm caused more damage than anything they had experienced previously and 747 mm rain fell in 24 hours. Houses collapsed and boats slipped their moorings and all the telegraph lines were brought down. Railways and bridges also suffered and you can see the state of the railway lines in the photo.

Ian sent another view of *Beagle* loading wool at Cossack Creek (top left) and with the tides here ships lie 'not always afloat but safely aground' (NAABSA in chartering terms).

Ian still remains in disagreement on the container point raised on page 62. He believes that, when it comes to the volume and economy of scale which are the secrets of the success of present-day container expansion, it was the Americans who pioneered this. He would not be surprised if the Phoenicians carried the odd container!

Photo 4/37
John Anderson notes that the strongback indicates former towing duties, but the radial davits port side aft now preclude towing. There is no capstan on deck for towing work (unless inside the house which was a North American practice); similarly there is a ladder in way of the capstan and no heavy bitts or tow hook. John thinks it might be a former tug/tender put to another use.

1/38. First a tug (above). A British-made postcard but with no creditation on the reverse side. The bulwarks are probably wood and the bridge may have been rebuilt.

2/38. A passenger liner with A.25 on her after-quarter (right). There are two notes on the back written in different hands. The first 'Australian Transport' and the second 'at Mudros or Gallipoli'.

127

3/38. Professor Theodore Siersdorfer from Germany sent the above pictures in the hope that we can help with identification. There is no doubt the first picture (above left) was supplied by John York of Bristol and taken by him - the original card has a message from him dated 9th June 1918. Bristol Museum has been unable to help. The name of the ship probably has six or seven letters.

4/38 The message on the second picture was written in Bari, Italy on 11th March 1929. Theodor thinks the photo may be of the Italian steamer *Marco*, ex *Capac*, completed 1893 for the New York and Pacific Steamship Co. Ltd. of London. She ended her days when broken up in Italy in 1932 as the *Marco*. Has anyone photos of her under either name for comparison?

5/38. A view in a shipbuilding or ship reparing yard. The ship next to the quay is the *Wyandotte*. The name of the smaller ship, nearer to the camera, can be seen but not read. It appears to have two parts with five and nine letters respectively.

6/38. A water-logged sailing ship (above) is towed into port. No indication on the photograph who took it but is it Dover in the background? Perhaps one of our south eastern readers can confirm this. Someone may have seen this or a similar view where the ship has been named.

7/38. At first sight a two-funnelled steamer but closer inspection shows two ships alongside each other. What is the one nearest to the camera which appears to be in the process of being repainted in a lighter colour?